Nosing & Tasting the Water of Life

Nosing & Tasting the Water of Life

Blue Collar & Scholar Guide to Whisky Pairing

Gregory J. Cran

J. Adam Drummond

Publication

Nosing & Tasting the Water of Life: Blue Collar & Scholar Guide to Whisky Pairing
Gregory J. Cran and J. Adam Drummond

Published in 2019
Blue Collar & Scholar Publication
www.bluecollarandscholar.com

Cover design by Nicole Narbonne, Skeenastreetstudio.ca.

Cover Photo by Gregory Cran – Royal Lochnagar Distillery, Aberdeenshire, Scotland

National Library of Canada Cataloging in Publication

ISBN: 978-1-9990067-0-9

1. Title. 2. Scotch Single Malt Whisky. 3. Scottish History. 4. Whisky Distilling. 5. Whisky Science. 6. Whisky Pairing. 7. Alchemy of Tasting. 8. Language of Whisky. 9. Water of Life. 10. Whisky Regions of Scotland. 11. Pronunciation guide of Scottish distilleries.

TABLE OF CONTENTS

FOREWORD

Blue Collar & Scholar is a pairing of my son and my husband who together have a passion for the discovery, comradery and sharing of a good whisky. Adam, who is 'blue collar' in this relationship, is a heavy events athlete (one who throws cabers and stones) and a certified automotive mechanic.

Greg is the scholar and a university principal and Whisky Ambassador with a passion for history, science and lore of the water of life. And, then there is me – I'm Wendy who has had the pleasure of serving many roles including fellow researcher and taster, tech support and task-master to keep their grasshopper minds in line to finish what they start out to do.

Historically, to be honest, I had always considered whisky to be booze, until I had my own epiphany when Greg and I took our first trip to Scotland and toured the Royal Lochnagar Distillery in Aberdeenshire. Here, I learned about an ancient practice and artistry of mashing, milling, fermenting, distilling and maturing this amazing spirit. The epiphanic moment came when I first experienced the nosing and tasting of a small dram that took twelve years to mature. And, in this moment I began to understand what all the fuss was about. I am a convert now - not a drinker, but a noser and sipper. For me, nosing and sipping means, not just enjoying, but appreciating this 'water of life' by experiencing the journey alongside my son and my husband.

Their story is about discovering and honouring the 'water of life' and with it a unique experience of sensory exploration.

What I learned is that the scent molecules of the whisky releases its own history that connects with what we bring to the moment. The scent can even trigger a certain memory or emotion. And, with each nosing a new sensory expression surfaces and launches yet another memory, leaving the prospect of more to come.

> *While we were visiting the Isle of Skye, one afternoon we had an opportunity to experience the warm and inviting smell of a peat fire burning in the fireplace of an old crofter cottage. The wind from the Atlantic Ocean was howling that day and the impact of the peat fire – both the warmth and the scent of the burning peat – conjured up the intensity of a past way of life and how this became refuge and comfort for survival.*
>
> *That evening we had our first dram of Talisker (Storm) at a local pub in Portree and were immediately transported back to the warmth and inviting smell of the peat fire experienced earlier in the day.*
>
> *Since then, each time we pour a dram of Talisker the smell and taste activate the warm memories of being back on the Isle. The brine, the smoke with hints of caramel and Christmas pudding are part of the allure. But interestingly, we do not get the same response from any other peated whiskies. A truly amazing moment for the curious-minded.*

This is the beginning. Their story is about discovering what complements the 'water of life' or *uisge beatha* as the Ancient Celts called it.

Slàinte,

Wendy Drummond

ONE

THE WATER OF LIFE

If you can look a dram in the whites of its ayes, while your nose reconnoitres with the rim of the glass and your lips take refuge like a well in search of a leak – then the whisky is ready… and so are you.

According to the Scottish Whisky Association, the whisky export industry in Scotland today is worth about £4.36bn ($7.59 billion) and directly employs about 10,000 people. Recent industry growth for single malt has been so significant that Scotland has had to import barley from England, Europe and Canada to keep up with demand. This means that more Scotch whisky is consumed around the world than Canadian, American and Irish whiskies combined. How did Scotch, which started as a small illicit cottage industry back in the 15th and 16th Century, grow so large? And, what is the appeal that has sustained its popularity to this day?

If we look back to the late 19th Century, global success of Scotch was due to the hard work and marketing prowess of a group of Scottish grocers, like Johnnie Walker, James Chivas, Tommy Dewar and others, who travelled European and North American continents seeking new markets. But like most market economies, whisky went through its own series of boom and bust cycles since that time.

In the late 1800s, for instance, the market collapse was due to greed followed by prohibition and two world wars in the early to mid-1900s. The second collapse in the market that occurred during the 1970s and 80s was influenced by an oversupply, an economic recession, and a baby boomer shift away from traditional spirits to lighter drinks. As a result, many of the smaller distilleries closed.

In the last ten years, the Scotch whisky industry has been experiencing its latest boom, with mothballed distilleries being reopened and many new distilleries now being built. This means that distillers are introducing new product lines and experimenting with different casks, such as wine, beer, port, rum and Champagne to help mature the next batch of whiskies. However, new whisky entrepreneurs are emerging outside of Europe and North America, with new single malt whiskies produced in Japan, India and Taiwan now capturing global interest.

The challenge for any whisky producer, be they from Scotland or elsewhere, is forecasting what the next generation of consumer will be craving and what lifestyle choices will influence their spending decisions. This is important given that today's production, using current methods and practices, won't be available for at least another six to eight years or more. While the industry figures this out, our goal is to discover what is it about the whisky experience that draws the interest it has.

An E or not an E

Why do the Irish and the Americans add an 'e' to the spelling of whiskey, while Scotland and the rest of world does not? Some claim the difference is due to the Irish thinking that the Scottish whisky was of lesser quality, while others claim it comes from differing Scottish and Irish translations of the term *Uisge Beatha*, what the ancient Celts called the 'water of life'.

Some differences between the two occurs during production. Irish whiskey is made from a blend of malted barley and unmalted barley in a single pot still or in some cases mixed with other grains. The reason is that back in the 1800s Irish distillers were having to pay malt taxes. Blending unmalted with malted barley was their way of reducing the tax burden.

Although Irish and Scottish whiskies are both distilled in copper pot stills and matured in oak casks for a minimum of three years, the main difference is that Scotch is known for being double distilled and Irish whiskey triple distilled allowing for a smoother tasting whiskey.

Although Irish whiskey was at one time the most popular whisk[e]y throughout the trading world, their popularity declined as far back as 1838 when Theobald Mathew, an Irish Catholic priest,established the Teetotal Abstinence Society which sparked the beginning of the temperance movement in Ireland. This was followed by the Irish Potato famine in 1845 leaving many to die in its wake or abandon Ireland for places abroad.

During this time, Ireland lost an estimated 70 distilleries and by 1916's Easter Rising and the War of Independence that followed, the decline in British trade cost Irish distillers their primary market. As for North American markets, World War II and American prohibition stifled trade leaving only a handful of distilleries to remain.

Since 1987 Irish whiskey has been experiencing a turnaround that has led to the emergence of many new distilleries and today is one of the fastest growing markets in the world.

As for the Americans and why their Bourbon whiskey is spelled with an 'e', it is told that the Irish were the first to introduce whiskey when they immigrated to the United States. (The exceptions being those like Maker's Mark Kentucky Straight Bourbon Whisky that goes against the grain of adding the 'e', paying homage to the Scottish heritage).

Blended or Single Malt Whisky

For clarity, whisky is made by mashing, fermenting and distilling various types of grains, such as barley, wheat, corn or rye, for making whisky. The resulting distillate is then matured in wooden casks, typically American or European oak.

Scotch whisky is produced and matured for a minimum of three years in Scotland. Scotch is either: 1) *single malt* made from 100% malted barley in pot stills at a single distillery*; 2) blended malt* made from a 100% barley malt whisky that is blended with two or more other malts from different distilleries; 3) *single grain* that uses any grain other than malted barley and distilled at a single distillery; 4) *blended Scotch*, which makes up about 90 percent of Scotch whiskies, is a blend of grain and malt whiskies from two or more distilleries.

Understanding & Appreciating the Water of Life

For this guide, we focussed on single malt Scotch, which by law must be made of malted barley, aged for a minimum of three years plus a day, and produced at a single distillery in Scotland.

Why single malt Scotch? Single malt is made from the traditional process of using pot stills, yeast and malted barley for producing the 'water of life' with nothing further added. With each single malt we believe there is an existential relationship between this ancient distilling tradition and a sensorial experience waiting to unfold.

Why Scotland? Well for a start, Scotland is a country full of mystery, whose culture and language is wrapped in myth and legend; and curiously enough has a unicorn for their national animal and a thistle as their national flower.

We see Scotland's whisky representing the link between these two national symbols – prickly for those who are not ready and ethereal for others who are. Each dram comes with its own romantic tale.

No doubt that whisky has played a part in exciting the warrior in some, but it has also been used to settle the warrior within, by serving as a catalyst for resolving complex clan issues.

> *About 1500 years ago, Scottish clansmen who were locked into a dispute were sent to Eilean a' Chomhraidh, the 'Island of Discussion' in Glencoe, Scotland to work out their differences. Here, feuding parties were left on the island alone with nothing but whisky, cheese and oatcakes. As the story is told, they didn't leave the island until the conflict was settled.*

If we are truly to learn from our past, there may be something to this story that has possibilities for managing our new world disorder. And, perhaps, whisky (along with cheese and oatcakes) can play a role in helping to address today's global issues. We leave it to your imagination to figure out the rest.

Using the Guide

Ask anyone about his or her whisky experience and you will get plenty of responses that range from being the worst experience in their life to discovering heaven on earth. We cannot assure that you will experience the 'heaven on earth', but we are willing to share what we have discovered and learned from others we had the opportunity to talk with.

Our journey began by asking friends, acquaintances, whisky tasting groups, bartenders, and 'nosers and spitters' who enjoy their single malt, what whiskies they prefer and why, and what they like to pair it with?

For a few, they relate to the image of old men sitting in an oversized leathery chair enjoying a large cigar with their Scotch. But for most, we learned that they chose a whisky that aligns with their moods, immerses their soul in sunsets, rain and fog or complements listening to music or reading a book. Some chose a certain whisky to celebrate events like caber tossing and stone throwing (and other athletic feats). And for others, such as writers and artists, they chose a whisky that helped unlock the muse, whether working online, in journals or with paints, clay or fibre. Although people's choice of whisky and what they pair it with was our focus, the highlight for us were the stories behind what people shared.

This guide begins with a brief history of how whisky made its way to Scotland and outwits gougers for hundreds of years. In Chapter Three, we set out the process of distilling the single malt. In Chapter Four, we describe the whisky regions and where the distilleries are located. We offer some science and lore in Chapter Five and in Chapter Six we explore the alchemy of tasting the 'water of life' or *uisge beatha* (oosh-ga-beh-ha) as the Ancient Celts called it or *Aqua Vitae,* as referred to by the monastics.

In Chapter Seven, we explore the language of whisky and the terms used in tasting and profiling the single malt. In Chapter Eight, we begin the pairings, first with food and then in Chapter Nine we pair with cigars, followed by activities and sunsets in Chapters Ten and Eleven. Finally, in Chapter Twelve we sum up with what we call 'e-valuating for the future'. This is where we explore the challenges we see facing the industry.

We also offer short vignettes throughout. And, for those who like their Scotch, but have no idea how to pronounce the names of the distilleries, we offer a little help in that direction as well. So, grab your dram and enjoy the journey.

TWO

BRIEF HISTORY

Figure 1From Oral to Text

Stories about Scottish history began as oral traditions, shared through song and poems by wandering bards throughout the Highlands and Lowlands. Many of these stories were collected by Sir Walter Scott, Robert Burns and many others, thus finding their way into the written text. What is myth and what are facts contained within these stories have been and will continue to be an ongoing debate.

The oldest documented reference to whisky occurs in the Scottish Exchequer Rolls of 1494, where there is an entry of "eight bolls of malt to Friar John Cor wherewith to make aqua vitae". (Friar Cor was a Tironensian monk and chief distiller at Lindores Abbey in the Kingdom of Fife).

How this 'water of life' came to Scotland remains a mystery to unravel. Some might argue that it was as far back as the 12th to 13th Century when the whisky arrived on the shores of Scotland and Ireland from the European continent, but where did the distillation process begin?

If we look at the history of distillation, there is prior evidence of crudely distilled alcoholic beverages made from rice and mare's milk in Asia as far back as 800 B.C. India, for instance, created a drink called Arrack, meaning distillate. Arrack, unlike Scottish whisky, was made from coconut flowers, red rice and sugar cane, producing a concoction intended for happy hour in ancient times. Not surprisingly, this distilled alcohol began to spread throughout South Asia, Egypt and Turkey. But it wasn't until the 8th century A.D. that Arabic alchemist Abu Musa Jabir ibn Hayyan designed the alembic pot still that allowed for the effective distillation of alcohol. Presumably, he designed the still to create finer essences of perfume rather than whisky. But once the monasteries got a hold of it (like coffee which was supposedly first introduced in Ethiopia through experimentation by monks), monasteries began experimenting with grains to produce their own distillate, which was referred to as *aqua vitae*. Through the spread of Christianity this water of life eventually made its way to Scotland and Ireland.

In 1505, James IV of Scotland, considered a Renaissance man with an active interest in alchemy, helped establish the Guild of Surgeon Barbers in Edinburgh and in the same year issued them an exclusive license to manufacture *aqua vitae*. This license essentially banned the production of this raw spirit for anything other than medicinal purposes (and possibly a good hair cut).

Between 1536 and 1541, King Henry VIII inadvertently influenced the expansion of whisky distilling with the dissolution of monasteries, nunneries and friaries in England, Wales and Ireland leaving unemployed monastics to fend for themselves without support of the church. Many applied their knowledge of distilling to help generate income by secretly introducing stills throughout the Highlands and the Islands.

To take advantage of this emerging industry, in 1644 the Scottish Parliament passed an Excise Tax that imposed taxes on whisky to replenish government coffers that were bled dry from a succession of battles over many years. This led to small distillers relocating their operations to rural areas that were less visible to avoid paying taxes.

The earliest reference to an actual distillery was in 1690 Acts of the Scottish Parliament when the famous Ferintosh distillery, owned by Duncan Forbes of Culloden, was mentioned. Forbes, a supporter of government, had his distillery burned down the year prior (1689) by the Jacobites. To compensate for his loss, Duncan Forbes was granted the right by the Scottish Parliament to distil free of duty.

Ferintosh whisky was the favoured drink among the Scots due to its drinkability and inexpensive price. During this time, the distillery was producing almost two-thirds of legally produced whisky in Scotland. Even Bonnie Prince Charlie was reputed to have drowned his sorrows in Ferintosh whisky after the Jacobite defeat at Culloden in 1746, which is ironic given that it was his supporters that had set the distillery ablaze.

Shortly after the Union of the Scottish and English Parliaments in 1707, there were numerous attempts by the English to control whisky production. With excise laws in disarray and industrial development on the rise, illicit distilling flourished. By 1777, there were about eight licensed distilleries in the Scottish Lowlands and 400 illegal ones in the Highlands.

To address illicit distilling, in 1784 the *Wash Act* was passed by the British parliament. This Act was an attempt to stimulate legal distilling in the Highlands and to lower duties for distilleries in the Lowlands and in England. The Act revoked Duncan Forbes right to distill free of duty at his Ferintosh distillery, which had the effect of leveling the field for the Highland distillers.

The Act created what was known as the 'Highland line', which was a line to separate the Lowlands from the Highlands by creating different excise levels. The Highlands were charged duty on the capacity of the still and the Lowlands were taxed on the amount produced. The Act also limited the Highland distilleries to a maximum of one 30-gallon still per district and only from grain grown in the Parish. Additionally, whisky that was made could only be consumed in the local area.

The Act did nothing to appease the Highlanders who were outraged at the fines levied and, as well, outraged the Lowlanders for allowing distilling privileges to the Highlanders. A consequence of the *Wash Act* was an enormous increase in production in the Lowlands. A large percentage of these spirits were exported to England, which led to an uprising by the London gin distillers. This resulted in the British parliament passing the *Scotch Distillery Act* in 1786. The Act imposed an extra duty on spirits exported to England, making it more difficult for Lowland distilleries to operate in the English market.

This infuriated those like Robert Burns, whose letter in 1786 sent to the 45 Scottish representatives in the House of Commons castigated them for their lack of help. As noted in his poem "Earnest Cry and Prayer':

Scotland, my auld, respected mither!
Tho' whiles ye moistify your leather,
Till, whare ye sit on craps o' heather,

Ye tine your dam;
Freedom an' whisky gang thegither!
Take aff your dram!

Once again, parliament's attempts to legalize production failed.

Illicit Distilling

The world of illicit whisky-making fits very well with Highlanders who epitomized defiance; not wanting anything to do with paying taxes or complying, for the most part, with government laws. Typically, whisky distilling took place in the winter months when access to the Highlands was limited. This was when small distillers surreptitiously moved their whisky to the Lowland markets with ingenuity, cunning and intrigue. Sending a few casks strapped to a mule in one direction, as a decoy was one such story. And, when the Government troops and excisemen went to investigate, they sent the actual whisky in another direction undetected. Watchmen organized a hilltop-to-hilltop signalling system to keep an eye on approaching Excise officers who ventured into the area.

There were many creative measures undertaken to keep the Excise officers at bay. For instance, there was an illicit still hidden in the hillside heather of the Highlands that channelled its smoke underground from the peat fire to a cottage some 70 yards away so that it could be released through the chimney without arousing suspicion. On the Isle of Orkney, Magnus Eunson, a whisky smuggler, clergyman, and founder of Highland Park Distillery was best portrayed in Alfred Barnard's 'The Whisky Distilleries of the United Kingdom'.

Hearing that the Church was to be searched for whisky by a new party of excisemen, Eunson had all the kegs removed to his house, placed in the middle of an empty room and covered with a clean white cloth. As the officers approached after their unsuccessful

> *search in the church, Eunson gathered all his people round the whisky, which, with its covering of white, under which a coffin lid had been placed, looked like a bier. Eunson knelt at the head with the Bible in his hand and the others with their psalm books. As the door opened, they set up a wail for the dead, and Eunson made a sign to the officers that it was a death and one of the attendants' whispered "smallpox". Immediately the officer and his men made off as fast as they could and left the smuggler for some time in peace.*

Many years later, after a lengthy Royal Commission, the *Excise Act* of 1823 sanctioned legal distilling that included a much-reduced flat-rate still licence, with duty levied on the amount of spirit produced.

What makes this date interesting is that in 1822, King George IV was the first British Monarch to visit Scotland in 170 years. Sir Walter Scott organized the King's visit to Edinburgh. This event was marked by the introduction of the Highland tartan and kilt, which had been banned by the English following the Battle of Culloden (1746) and looked on with disdain by the Scottish Lowland gentry who considered the Highlanders 'savages'.

In celebrating the Monarch's arrival, Sir Walter Scott toasted the King's health with the finest Highland whisky, amusingly from Glenlivet, an illicit whisky produced in Highland bothies hidden in the hills, rather than one of the licensed Lowland distilleries. The King was so impressed he demanded more until the supply eventually ran dry.

The problem for the King was that there was none of this illicit whisky to be found in Edinburgh or any other parts of the Lowlands. So, coincidentally or not, a year later the *Excise Act* of 1823 sanctioned legal distilling with the help of Alexander Gordon the 4th Duke of Gordon whose tenant happened to be George Smith, who owned Glenlivet. In 1824, Glenlivet distillery was the first in northeastern Scotland to be legalized.

Legalizing Highland Distilling

When George Smith decided to proceed with his license, he endured numerous attacks, including threats to burn down his distillery by local illicit distillers and smugglers who were not happy with what he had done. To defend himself George carried a pair of pistols offered to him for protection by the Laird of Aberlour. As for the other Highland distillers, they eventually gave up resisting.

The number of licensed distilleries grew from one hundred and eleven in 1823 to two hundred and sixty-three in 1825, most of them small (under 500 gallons still capacity) and many by former smugglers with encouragement from their landlords. This represented an increase in volume from three million gallons in 1823 to ten million gallons by 1828.

After Glenlivet, the next to be won over to the licensing side was the Cardhu distillery (initially known as Cardow), located nearby. John and Helen Cumming owned this small distillery. John, a noted whisky smuggler reportedly convicted three times for distilling without a licence, had a farm distillery with his wife Helen and daughter-in-law Elizabeth, both of whom served as the distillers. Before receiving their license, neighbours and other illicit distillers in the area would watch for a red flag flying above the Cumming's farm, which was Helen's way of signalling everyone that an Excise officer was in the area, thus putting all sales on hold. Shortly after they became legitimate, other Highland distillers realized that there was more to be made from entering the market than concealing what they crafted.

Introducing the Continuous Still

In 1832, the Coffey still (also referred to as the continuous still or column still), was patented by Aeneas Coffey, former Inspector General of Excise in Dublin. A year later, the first Coffey still was installed in Scotland at the Grange distillery in Fife. The Coffey still revolutionized the whisky industry by introducing the process for continuous distillation of grain whisky. This allowed for less expensive and more efficient whisky production and in greater volume. Although Coffey initially introduced this new style still in Ireland, there were no Irish takers and hence he moved his still to the Lowlands of Scotland.

With the new Coffey still, grains other than barley could be used to make whisky. However, the whisky was rather weak compared to what people were used to, so blending this grainy distillate with pot still whisky in local cellars was introduced by Victorian grocers, such as the Walkers from Kilmarnock in Ayrshire, Dewars and Bells from Perth, and the Chivas brothers from Aberdeen who bottled and sold this blended whisky in their stores.

With the advent of railways and modern bottling techniques, these blends made their way into a growing export market. By the end of the Victorian era, the demand for Scotch whisky boomed, but not without a little help from an aphid in France.

Collapse of the French Brandy and Wine Industry

In the 1860s, a voracious aphid called phylloxera that destroyed many of the vineyards in France had devastated the French brandy and wine industry. Over 40% of the French vines and vineyards were destroyed over a fifteen-year period. This event created havoc for the English aristocracy who were ardent Cognac and brandy drinkers and for the English middle class who enjoyed their wines.

The English were not Scotch drinkers, largely due to the lack of quality and standards at the time. So, in 1886 Alfred Barnard, as Secretary of Harper's Weekly Gazette, visited all the whisky distilleries in Scotland of which there were 129 at the time. He also visited 29 more in Ireland and 4 in England and reported his findings in his book 'The Whisky Distilleries of the United Kingdom'. Although intrigued and supportive with what he found, many brandy drinkers found the whisky a bit unpalatable and turned to Sherry instead.

Sherry was shipped to England in transport casks and bottled in London. Due to the high costs of returning the casks to Spain, these casks were sold to the Highland distilleries that were delighted to use them for maturing their young whiskies. Sherry matured whisky resulted in a smoother more drinkable whisky. With the rise of blended whiskies, consistency and quality of this new whisky pacified the brandy drinkers. Hence, the whisky market boomed.

By the mid-1890s, investment in whisky had become very trendy with huge loans invested in Scotch whisky stocks. However, by the late 1890s, shady financial practices by independent bottlers became commonplace. One such bottler – Pattison, Elder & Company – was particularly noteworthy, according to whisky historian Gavin D. Smith. "This was a company that started out as a dairy wholesaler in Edinburgh and, like many, entered the whisky business to seek greater profit. Unfortunately, they resorted to underhand tactics to inflate the value of their stock". This helped trigger a cascade of closures throughout the Scottish whisky industry. The Pattison firm declared bankruptcy, along with nine other companies they had partnered with at the time. In 1901, the Pattison brothers were convicted on four counts of fraud and embezzlement. This was known as the 'Pattison Crash', which was the beginning of some tough times for the whisky industry. World War

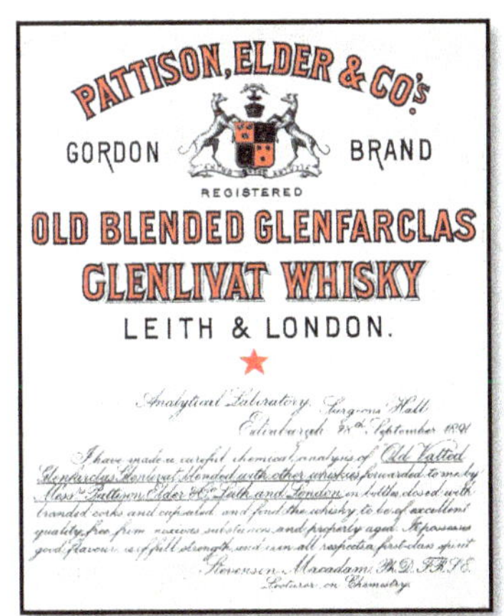

Figure 2 Pattison Crash

I came soon after, followed by American Prohibition and World War II. Yet the industry survived, with the next boom taking place at the end of the World War II.

After American prohibition and World War II ended, the Bourbon industry in the southern United States started to produce Bourbon again. The Cooperage union, which constructed the barrels used for aging whiskey, had closed during prohibition and the war years. When the Bourbon industry started up again the Cooperage union made a deal with the industry that Bourbon casks could only be used once. This created a large supply of used casks, which was timely as the Spanish Civil War and WWII caused Sherry production to come to an abrupt halt, which meant a lack of Sherry casks at a time when the whisky industry had just begun to re-emerge.

Today, Bourbon casks make up about 90% of all casks used for maturing young Scottish whiskies.

Data from Her Majesty's Revenue and Customs shows that Scotch whisky exports totalled $7.59 billion in Canadian dollars, which equates to 1.7 billion bottles. Scotch, alone, accounts for 20 percent of all the United Kingdom's food and drink exports. The increase in volume and sales is due to the rise of single malt.

> *The first drink I ever ordered at a restaurant was scotch and soda (wanting to sound grown up as I was underage at the time), and it was horrid and left me wondering what the hell people were thinking.*
>
> *Today, as I write this, I am enjoying a dram of Highland Park 18 year and reflecting on how far I had come. Is it age that brings us to a new awareness and appreciation? I am not sure, but I do know that the floral smell with a slightly heathery peat and honey taste, reminds me of where I have been.*

THREE

DISTILLING PROCESS

Figure 3 Distillery Operations

Making whisky is a long and enduring process that brings traditional distilling practices together with science, artistry and engineering. The making of single malt starts with barley gathered from local farms or purchased from commercial barley producers located in different parts of Scotland.

Malting

The traditional malting process begins when barley is steeped in water for a day or two and then left to germinate on the malting floor (usually about a week). Germination of the barley stimulates the production of enzymes that transform the starch in the barley into sugars.

Figure 4 Malting Floor

Once sprouted, the barley is dried in a kiln to eliminate moisture and halt the germination process before milling. Peat, which is decomposed vegetation found in bogs and harvested for heat throughout the Highlands and Islands, is used by some distillers to heat the kiln, while others use gas or coal. The peat adds a smoky, sometimes salty medicinal flavour to the barley - depending on the amount of peat used and where it was harvested. Nowadays, for most distilleries, due to large-scale demand, malting is done at a commercial malting facility.

Milling

After the malt is dried, it is ground in a mill into grist, husks and flour. The result is 70 percent grist, 20 percent husk and 10 percent flour. This breakdown is essential for the mashing stage to work efficiently.

Mashing

From here, the grist is mixed with hot water in a large stainless steel called a mash tun. This is where the mix is agitated so the starch in the grist can convert into sugar by the action of the enzymes, producing a sugary liquid called wort. The wort is released through a perforated base in the mash tun.

Figure 5 Mash Tun

The quality of the wort, whether cloudy or clear, affects the flavour. For instance, a cloudy wort containing husks and flour from the barley will produce a nutty, malty, more cereal character compared to a clear wort.

The quantity and quality of the wort also determines the amount of alcohol produced at the end of the process.

Fermenting

Figure 6 Pot Stills with Lyne arms

Once the wort is cooled, it is pumped into fermenting vessels called washbacks made from either wood (Oregon pine) or stainless steel. This is when yeast is added to the liquid to allow for fermentation, converting the sugars in the wort into alcohol. This takes about 48 hours. The resulting clear liquid is referred to as the wash.

Although ready to be distilled, there are some distilleries that let the wash undergo further fermentation by leaving it sit for an additional twelve hours or more. In doing so, this adds more complex floral and fruity flavours.

Distilling

The distilling process begins when the wash is transferred from the washbacks to the first of two copper pot stills – the first - called the wash still is where the wash (about 8% alcohol-by-volume) is brought to a boil.

As the mash is heated, the liquid vaporizes and rises through the neck of the still. As it rises, the vapour begins to condense and falls back into the still. Eventually as

Figure 7 Lyne Arm

the liquid temperature increases to 78C it rises into the neck and through the lyne arm, a long protruding pipe, then into the condenser where it condenses the vapours into liquid. This process takes somewhere between 4 to 7 hours.

Before transferring the spirit into the second still or 'spirit still', the spirit is now referred to as low wines with an alcohol level of about 23% abv (alcohol-by-volume). Here, the low wine passes first into a tank where it mixes with what was left (called fractions) from a previous distillation.

The initial fractions are referred to as foreshots that are very high in alcohol and very pungent as well. The other fractions are called ends or feints and although not as high in alcohol they too are very pungent. The desired alcohol collected is from the middle or heart of the distillation. This leaves an alcoholic strength of about 65 to 70% abv.

After the process is repeated in the spirit still, the second distillation process collects the hearts of the spirit (about 60% alcohol) now referred to as 'new make spirit'.

Before the clear spirit is poured into oak casks to begin the aging and maturation process, the spirit is inspected through a window in a secured brass and glass wall called a spirit safe.

Figure 8 Spirit Safe

The spirit safe was historically locked and only accessed by Customs and Excise men, which prevented the distiller from siphoning off the spirit to avoid paying duty. Now, with less controls, the process allows for inspection by the distiller to determine the readiness of the new make spirit prior to maturing.

Maturing

The last step in the distillation process is to mature the 'new make spirit' in casks. These casks are made from oak that in most cases has been previously used for storing Bourbon or Sherry (or more recently wine or virgin casks) for a minimum of three years and often finished in a second cask (or a third or possibly more) to complement the first.

Casks come in different sizes depending on their place of origin. For example, American oak barrels are 200 litres that are often remade into larger casks called hogsheads, which hold 250 litres. European oak casks, called butts or puncheons, hold 500 litres. Some distillers are now using smaller casks or quarter casks (50 litres), which allows the whisky to mature more rapidly.

Figure 9 Casks used for maturation

To meet the legal requirements of Scotch whisky, the whisky must mature in the cask for a minimum of three years or more accurately, three years plus a day. During this maturation process, evaporation occurs at about 1.5 to 2 percent per year on average, depending on various factors, such as climate and warehousing. This means that over a ten-year period the volume of the cask is reduced by about 15 to 20 percent (and more for whiskies matured for longer periods). This is referred to in the industry as the 'angel's share'. If one calculates the angel's share throughout all of Scotland, this equates to a loss of about 150 million bottles per year through evaporation. Clearly, this allows angels to be light on their wings.

The benefit of using multiple casks for finishing adds to the taste profile of the whisky. Although maturation in the cask represents about 60 to 70 percent of the overall taste, other steps in the distilling process that influence the flavour profile of whisky include: type of barley and where it is grown, the climate and location of the distillery, the quality and purity of the water, the height and shape of the stills, and the angle of the lyne arm. Each, in its own way, contributes to the aromatics; how it performs on the palate; and, how it finishes - in preparation of the tasting experience.

> *Measuring Proof*
>
> *In early times, a test for telling whether the whisky was ready for drinking was when the distiller added a pinch of gunpowder to the spirit. If the flame was bright, the whisky was "proof", meaning the alcohol content was right. If the flame was bluish and weak, it was "under proof". If the mixture exploded, it was "over proof". This took the pluckiest of souls to ignite the mixture because if the whisky exploded you not only risked life and limb, but you ended up with a whisky even the most hardened would find difficult to drink.*
>
> *Today, thanks to more modern technology, we have different means to tell whether the whisky is suited for drinking, far removed from the gunpowder days.*

Figure 10 Proof is in the glass

FOUR

WHISKY REGIONS OF SCOTLAND

There are five official whisky-distilling regions in Scotland, defined by The Scottish Whisky Regulations of 2009. These regional names include: Lowlands, Highlands, Speyside, Islay, and Campbeltown. However, numerous authors have chosen to add 'Islands' as a sixth category, rather than include the island distilleries under 'Highlands'. Islands include distilleries located on Orkney, Skye, Mull, Arran, Lewis, Harris and Jura each of whom add their own distinctiveness and expression to the single malt.

Currently, according to the Scotch Whisky Association, there are 126 licensed distilleries in Scotland with new distilleries coming into production each year.

The Lowlands

In the 1800s, there were over 200 licensed malt distilleries in the Lowlands, which represented the southernmost area of Scotland. Lowland distilleries were licensed and taxed, in contrast to the many illicit distilleries hidden in the Highlands of Scotland.

It was in 1823 when the *Excise Act* was proclaimed and distilleries throughout Scotland were licensed. This is when Lowland distilleries had to compete with the Highlands heathery hills and crystal-clear water. This may be a reason (along with the spread of urbanization) that only four active distilleries in the Lowlands remained. Lowland whiskies, like Auchentoshan and Glenkinchie, are known for their light mellow character, with its floral and cereal malty taste. Distilleries in the Lowlands include GlenKinchie, south of Edinburgh, Ailsa Bay in Girvan, Auchentoshan near Glasgow and Bladnoch in Galloway. All are unpeated, producing a very smooth whisky. Unlike most distilleries in Scotland, Auchentoshan triple distills its whisky like many, if not most, of the distilleries in Ireland.

The Highlands

Prior to the introduction of the *Excise Act* of 1823, unlicensed Highland distilleries operated with impunity, if they didn't try to sell their whisky outside their parish or region. However, many found it more lucrative to smuggle their whisky to the south where the higher quality Highland malt was in demand, which required ingenuity and creativity to succeed in getting their product to market.

In the mid-1800s, when the Lowland distilleries began producing grain whiskies using Coffey stills, the Highlands continued to produce malt whisky. But rather than producing single malts, Highland whiskies, being typically less sweet and more robust, were blended with other grain whiskies helping to make blended whisky more palatable.

Geographically, the Highlands are the largest distillery-making region in Scotland. The central part of the Highlands stretches from Inverness to Perth. Perth was once considered the 'blending capital' of Scotland, given its favourable geographic position that provided easy access to the Highland malts and the Lowland grain whisky, and to the lucrative export markets as well.

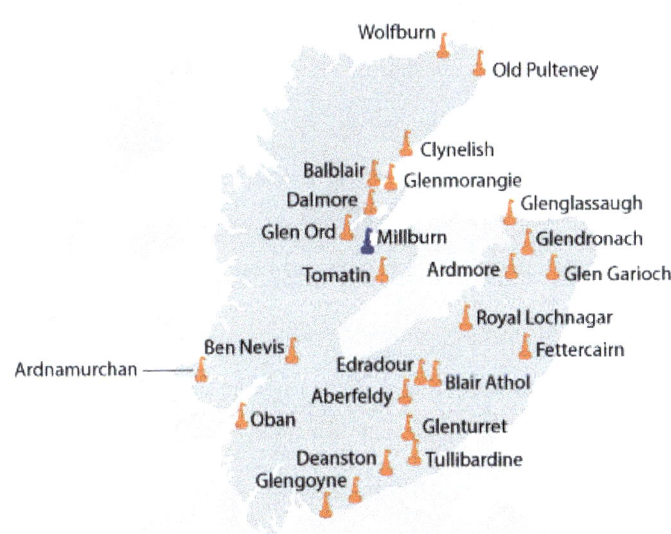

Central Highland distilleries include Tomatin, Dalwhinnie, Blair Athol, Edradour, Aberfeldy, Glenturret, Tullibardine, Deanston, and Glengoyne. Single malts from this part of the Highlands are considered sweeter and more fragrant than other distilling regions.

North Highlands extends from Inverness north with most of the distilleries located on the coast, the exception being the Glen Ord distillery that is located inland, north east of Inverness. These whiskies are noted for their saltiness, sometimes spicy with a tinge of light smoke. North Highland distilleries include Old Pulteney, Glenmorangie, Wolfburn, Clynelish, Balbair, Dalmore, and Glen Ord.

Eastern Highland single malts are derived from a rich and fertile countryside that stretches east of the River Spey and Grampian Mountains to Montrose on the southern east coast. At one time, the City of Aberdeen had twelve distilleries of which none have survived. Eastern malts are considered medium to full-bodied with a dry finish that can, in some cases, be slightly smoky, with toffee, ginger and citrus expressions depending on whether the whisky has been matured in Bourbon or Sherry or a combination of the two. Distilleries, like Glendronach, are noted for Sherry casks to enhance their flavour. Distilleries in this area include Knockdhu, Glendronach, Glen Garioch, Royal Lochnagar, and Fettercairn.

Western Highlands has two distilleries - Ben Nevis near Fort William and Oban located on the west coast. Distilling here is done on a smaller scale as barley crops were not easy to grow due to heavy rainfall and less productive agricultural land. Ben Nevis is noted for its sweet butterscotch and spice with a bit of nuttiness. Oban, on the other hand, has more of a maritime and fresh fruit flavour profile.

Speyside

In North Eastern Scotland, stretching from the River Findhorn to the east side of the River Spey, is an area, known as Speyside, which has the largest concentration of distilleries in Scotland. Historically, Speyside was an isolated area of the

Highlands attractive to illicit distillers wishing to be free of rules, taxes and regulations.

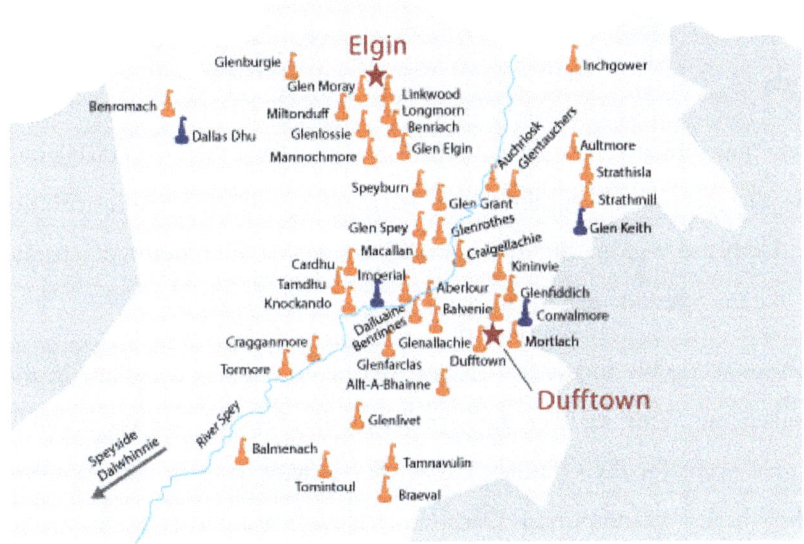

Until the 1823 *Excise Act* was proclaimed, there were only two licensed distilleries in the Speyside region and two hundred illicit stills in Glenlivet parish alone. By the mid-1880s, there were twenty-three distilleries built to meet the rising demand for malt whisky. Whiskies from this area are known for their quality and smoothness and range from light to full-bodied that is usually unpeated.

The reason there are so many whisky distilleries in this area is largely due to the abundance and quality of water, as it takes about 50 liters of water to produce one litre of whisky. The region's water has the lowest level of dissolved minerals than any other region in Scotland.

Notable distilleries include The Balvenie, Allt-a-Bhainne, Strathisla, Aberlour, Glen Moray, Glenfiddich, Cragganmore, Cardhu, The Glenlivet, Macallan, Benromach, BenRiach, Aultmore, Glen Grant, Tamdhu, Knockando, Glenfarclas, Mortlach and Glenrothes.

The Islands

Of the ninety-nine inhabited islands in Scotland, only six have their own distilleries. The Islands, the exception being the Isle of Islay, are typically lumped in with the rest of the Highland region. But many would argue that they deserve separate distinction like the Speyside region.

Although more accessible today, the islands were remote and accessibility in the past was challenging. Whiskies from the Islands tend to reflect harsher wet maritime environment. Except for the Orkneys, barley was difficult to grow and therefore much of their barley was imported. Despite the harsh wind and rains, the island winters were more forgiving, giving the whiskies their own distinctive character.

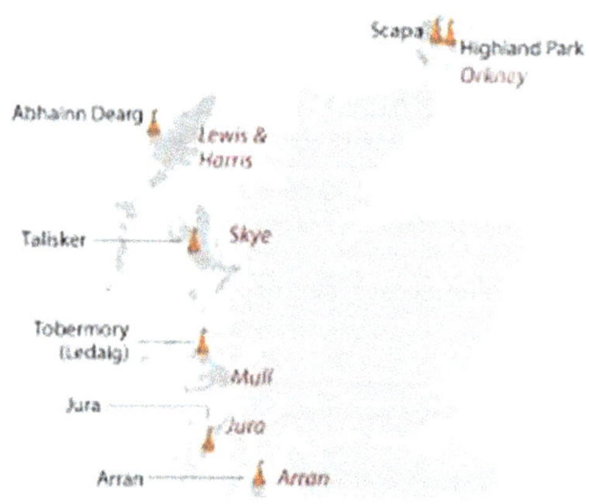

Notable island distilleries include Highland Park and Scapa in the Orkneys, Abhainn Dearg on Isle of Lewis and the new Isle of Harris Distillery, both located in the Outer Hebrides. In the Inner Hebrides, there is Talisker on the Isle of Skye, Arran on the Isle of Arran, Jura on Isle of Jura, and Tobermory on the Isle of Mull.

Isle of Islay

Islay is the most fertile island in the Hebrides. Its abundance of water and peat bogs provides the distinctive character to most of the whiskies produced on Islay. Islay's peat is different from the woody peat of the Highlands and the heathery peat of the Orkneys. Islay's peat contains a high moss content that absorbs the salty sea air and gives it a sweet and salty smell. Distilleries on Islay include Bowmore, Lagavulin, Laphroaig, Ardbeg, Bruichladdich, Caol Ila, Bunnahabhain, and Kilchoman. Kilchoman opened in 2005 and was the first distillery built on the island in 124 years. Ardnahoe is the latest addition to be opened and soon to be re-opened is Port Ellen in 2020.

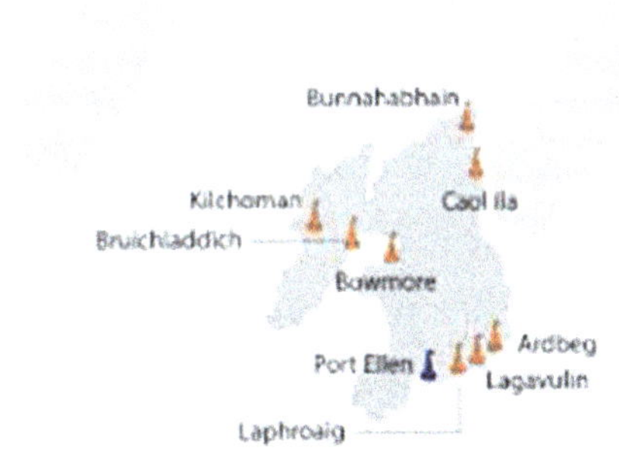

Campbeltown

Campbeltown, located on the Kintyre peninsula in south western Scotland, was considered at one time to be the whisky capital of Scotland with 34 distilleries, but after the First World War only three remained. The reason for decline was the over-production of whisky considered to be of lower quality, prohibition in the U.S, and a trend toward lighter 'Speyside' style of whiskies. However, that has changed with the three notable distilleries of Springbank, Glengyle, and Glen Scotia producing high quality, sought after malts.

The whisky regions are influenced by their unique climates, rugged landscapes and geographic locations. Whiskies draw their character, not only from distilling traditions and processes, but also from the flora, the water, the humidity, and the surrounding cultural anthropology in which distilleries are located. As Charles Maclean describes in 'Spirit and Place: Scotlands Great Whisky Distilleries', malt whisky is the quintessence of Scotland.

...it conjures the land of its birth in all its seasons with every sip – flowering machair in spring, warm beaches and heather pollen in summer, wayside berries and orchards in autumn, and the reek of winter peat...The smells of cooking and baking, childhood sweets, leather upholstery, grandpas's motor car, church candles, cut grass, meadows, pine forests, sawn timber...

FIVE

SCIENCE AND LORE

Scanning for evidence, capturing stories or toying with the muse can sometimes lead to unrealistic expectations, a grasshopper mind or the occasional ink stain swatches from a leaky fountain pen. In moments like these, the question is how to regain the muse to keep the ink flowing. For the darkest of times, a Lagavulin 16 or a Bruichladdich's Octomore 7.1, with its sweet smoke, brine, baking spices and iodine, makes a highly suited tourniquet for compressing wayward thoughts and keeping the grasshopper mind in line.

Colour of Whisky

The colour of whisky has often been considered a determinant of the age of the whisky. While whisky ranges from a pale yellow to a reddish and dark, the assumption is that the longer a spirit is aged in a cask the darker the whisky will appear.

Figure 11 Glencairn glass

The colour of whisky, however, is determined by several factors that include the length of time the spirit remains in the cask, whether the cask has been toasted or charred and the type of cask used e.g. Bourbon or Sherry, or virgin oak.

The challenge for the distiller is that casks do not produce a consistency in colour, as one cask may impart a slightly different hue from another due to how many times the cask has been used and other factors. This is where many distilleries compensate the colour inconsistencies by adding caramel colouring.

Caramel colouring is a product of burning sugars like fructose and glucose until they have turned into a dark syrup known as E150a (E stands for European). E150a (sometimes referred to as spirit caramel), unlike E150b (caustic sulfite caramel), E150c (ammonia caramel) or E150d (sulfite-ammonia caramel), is free of harmful chemicals or residue such as sulfates or ammonium and only a relatively small percentage is used for colour.

Most single malts and virtually all blended whiskies are coloured with E150a. The Scotch Whisky Regulations 2009 stipulates that the only ingredients that can be added to the whisky are water and caramel for colouring, not for flavour.

Is caramel colouring harmful, necessary or simply a vanity? Some in the industry claim it is only harmful when it comes to consumer perception. The Scotch whisky industry claims that adding caramel colouring improves the look and consistency, and by extension, the value of their whisky. However, more and more distilleries are becoming aware of the importance of public perception and its influences on a new generation of whisky consumer, noting that no coloring has been added.

Chill Filtration

When reading the label on some whiskies, there may be a reference to non-chill filtered. The purpose of chill filtering is to remove naturally occurring fatty acids, proteins and esters that are formed by enzyme reaction of yeast and alcohol during fermentation.

A non-chill filtered whisky that is 46% alcohol by volume (abv) or lower will go cloudy when ice is added or will develop sediment in the bottle when stored in a cool place. However, whiskies with an abv above 46% do not require chill filtration, as the higher alcohol level prevents this cloudiness from occurring. For whiskies bottled at 46 abv or lower, chill filtering eliminates the cloudiness these elements create when the whisky is cooled.

The chill filtration process involves dropping the temperature of the whisky to zero degrees Celsius for single malts (and -4 degrees for blends). Once chilled, the whisky is passed under pressure through a series of tightly knit metallic meshes or paper filters. The filtering process is also designed to remove other impurities from the cask during maturation that may be present.

The subject of chill filtration is an ongoing debate. Like caramel colouring, the main reason to chill filter a whisky is purely cosmetic and is designed to improve the presentation and appearance for the consumer. On one hand, there is the discerning consumer who desires more natural (or organic) products to complement their lifestyle choices. On the other hand, there are those in the industry who believe that consistency of colour assures quality. Arguably, chill filtration influences the aromatics profile when it eliminates esters, fatty acids and proteins through chill-filtration as these are some of the compounds that enhance the richness and complexity of the whisky.

Splash or no Splash

Should water be added to Scotch or should it not, has also been an ongoing debate. Bjorn Karlsson and Ran Friedman from Linnaeus University in Sweden decided to replicate what is found in a glass of single malt whisky to calculate the molecular motion. They added a single molecule of guaiacol, an aromatic chemical compound, to provide the Scotch's distinctive peaty and smoky flavour. Guaiacol is found in higher concentrations in certain Scotch whiskies more so than in Irish or American, especially when the malted barley, used in the fermentation process, is smoked over a peat fire.

What Karlsson and Friedman discovered is that when a whisky is at or above 40 percent alcohol by volume, guaiacol molecules tend to stay in the body of the liquid, away from the surface. But when the researchers diluted the simulated whisky to about 25 percent alcohol, the guaiacol floated to the top allowing its smoky and peaty scent to be easily drawn in by the nose.

Next, Karlsson and Friedman focussed their attention on the interaction between the water, guaiacol and ethanol. Here, they discovered that ethanol clusters guaiacol molecules into clumps. When Scotch is distilled, ethanol concentrations are as high as 59 percent, with aromatic guaiacol compounds attached. When diluted to roughly 40 percent, before bottling, ethanol accumulates near the surface accompanied by guaiacol. When ethanol levels are diluted to 27 percent, after a splash of water has been added, the ethanol and guaiacol aerosolize, enabling the fragrant peaty and smoky compounds to be more easily drawn in by the nose.

Knowing that taste and smell are linked, it may be worth noting that the right amount of water is needed to enhance the flavours. As water dilutes the whisky, ethanol spreads allowing more of the guaiacol to surface. However, there is a fine balance, as the author's note, "between diluting the whisky to taste and diluting the whisky to waste." Too much dilution, and you lose that aerosolizing effect.

Gently sloshing Scotch in its glass jostles the other phenols in the liquid loose, further enhancing its aroma. A splash of water can open new and subtle flavours that may not have been previously experienced. Here, a tulip-shaped glass, such as a Glencairn glass, funnels those molecules into the nostrils to enhance the aromatic complexities found in a good single malt Scotch. This is especially true of cask strength whiskies with their higher alcohol by volume levels. In short, every whisky is chock full of its own variety of aromatics and compounds that are unique to each distillery location and the process in which it was made.

Figure 12 Whisky glasses

Does Glassware Matter?

What is the ideal glass for 'drinking' single malt whisky, some often ask? Traditionally, you have the 'Old Fashioned' tumbler that is common in most bars and the tulip shape glass that is used at whisky tasting events. When ordering a single malt in a pub, typically it will come in a tumbler and appear lost due to the size of the glass and challenging when trying to distinguish the scent profile of the whisky.

Tulip shape glasses, with a narrower aperture at the brim, are ideal for nosing a single malt. Conversely, the tumbler, with its wide rim is better used with blended whiskies where ice and soda, cola, or Chinese green tea may be added. Their shortcoming is that the tumbler is only able to reflect the most aggressive notes, losing much of the subtle nuances.

Using different types of glasses creates different oxidation effects when the whisky comes into contact with the air. The wider the shoulder of the glass, the more surface contact the whisky has with the air, hence the faster the oxygenation.

For nosing and tasting, some whisky aficionados prefer a stemmed tulip shape glass to avoid heating the contents of the glass with their hand and to avoid any odours that the hand may give off. The tulip shape design allows for a concentration of scents. However, not every tulip shape glass has a stem and for those that don't there are many to choose from.

For example, the Glencairn glass with its narrow opening is an ideal snifter that nicely captures the aromas of the whisky. It also captures the ethanol and with a cask strength whisky of 48 percent (abv) or higher, this can be overwhelming. Here, adding a few drops of water to diffuse the alcohol clarifies the nosing. Some might argue that the narrow aperture of the brim of the Glencairn glass only allows enough room for the nose when sniffing or the lips when tasting, but not both together.

There are other glasses designed for whisky on the market that provide a slightly larger brim. Examples include the Riedel Vinum Single Malt Whisky Glass with its remarkably thin design. The NEAT glass (Naturally Engineered Aroma Technology) that looks like a flattened, wide belly version of the Glencairn. The NEAT is intended to redirect the harsh alcohol vapours away from the nose without having to add the splash of water. And, the Norlan glass, a double walled, hand-blown borosilicate glass. With the Norlan, you have a concave lip that fits both the lower lip and the nose that enables the whisky to be more expressive.

Assessing the Alcohol Content on the Glass

Observing the legs (or sometimes referred to as tears) of a whisky when one swirls the whisky in the glass, and the slowness with which they fall, enables you to assess or helps to indicate the alcohol content. These legs are the result of the difference in surface tension between the ethanol molecules and the water contained in the whisky. As surface tension is lower in alcohol than in water, the higher the alcohol content, the more legs there will be and the slower they will form and fall. As ethanol evaporates faster than water, the thin layer of whisky on the side of the glass that is exposed to air is extra watery. Whereas, more fatty acids, tannins and esters the whisky contains, the thicker these legs will appear.

Whisky: Medicinal or Simply Lore?

We frequently hear that a dram a day will extend one's life, but how much whisky's medicinal reputation is fact versus lore. The Celts considered *uisge beatha* to be medicinal, which prolonged life and provided relief for colicky infants, as well as those suffering from smallpox and a host of other ailments. In short, whisky was extensively used from the cradle to the grave, reviving tired bodies and providing pain relief, as well as welcoming travellers and other guests.

The famous chronicler Raphaël Holinshed recorded in his book the *Chronicles of England, Scotland and Ireland* in 1577, that whisky had certain advantages:

> Being moderately taken, it slows the age, cuts phlegm, helps digestion, cures the dropsy, it heals the strangulation, keeps and preserves the head from whirling, the tongue from lisping, the stomach from womblying, the guts from rumbling, the hands from shivering, the bones from aching…and truly it is a sovereign liquor if it be orderly taken.

Whisky was also being used as an antiseptic to clean wounds, when access to medical supplies was in short supply.

These medicinal references continued into the 20th century. One story told by Sean Murphy in an article in the Scotsman Food + Drink (2017),

> *During Prohibition in the 1920s, Scotch, could legally be imported into the United States because it was considered a medicine, not a liquor. "A person may, without a permit, purchase and use liquor for medicinal purposes when prescribed by a physician as herein provided."– Volstead Act [1920]. In 1919 and before Prohibition, Walgreens founder Charles R. Walgreen had around 20 stores, however, after Prohibition in 1929, the*

pharmacy expanded to well over 525 outlets, with much of this success reportedly being attributed to sales of whisky 'for medicinal consumption'.

In 1998, the Rowett Research Institute in Aberdeen conducted a study to assess whether the consumption of 100ml of 12-year-old whisky matured in oak casks, a 'new make' whisky recently distilled (not matured), or red wine increased phenolic content and antioxidant capacity of their plasma.

The research revealed that both the 12-year-old oak matured whisky and red wine helped to protect against coronary heart disease by raising the body's level of antioxidants. One such antioxidant is ellagic acid, a natural phenol found in numerous fruits and vegetables. Ellagic is present in North American white oak and European red oak barrels in which whisky is stored. These antioxidants help to counteract destructive chemicals in the blood known as free radicals, which hasten the ageing process and potentially damage tissue.

The 'new make' spirit, however, showed no change in phenolic plasma concentration. One might conclude that the longer the whisky is aged the greater the antioxidant capacity. However, that is the subject of future research.

In 1577, Raphael Holinshed published his Chronicles of England, Scotland and Ireland. In his Chronicles, Holinshed describes the medicinal effects of Aqua Vitae:

… It dryeth up the breaking up of the hands, and killeth the fleshe wormes, if you wash your hands therewith. Being moderately taken, sayth he, it sloeth age strengtheneth youth, it helpeth digestion, it cutteth fleume, it abandoned melancholy, it relisheth the hart, it lighteneth the mynd, it quickeneth the spirites, it cureth the hydropsie…it kepeth & preserveth the hed from whirlying, the eyes from dazelyng, the tongue from lispyng, the mouth from mafflyng, the teeth from chattering, the throte from rattling, the weasan from stieflyng, the stomach from wambling, the belly from wirtvhyng, the guts from rumbling, the hands from shivering, the veynes from crumplying, the bones from akying, the marrow from soakying, and truly it is a sovereign liquor if it be orderlie taken.

SIX

ALCHEMY OF TASTING

We were told that soaking a harmonica overnight in a dram of Scotch cleans the crud from the reeds and plays better for having imparted a 'whisky breath' to the wooden comb. Since neither Blue Collar nor Scholar plays the harmonica, we accept this sacrificial anointment at its word... arguably as a bit of lore! The question we have is more about the Scotch and whether it tastes better for having been the well for dunking.

Figure 13 Tasting room, Royal Lochnagar

The alchemy of whisky tasting is about exploring the varied expressions and intricate notes of the whisky. This requires a lot of patience and plenty of testing. Tasting itself is not only a sensory pleasure, but an analytical one, piecing together what is discovered through the nose and palate with memory. Nuances of sight, taste, texture, and smell of a whisky can move us from experiencing enjoyment to a new level – one of understanding and appreciation.

This is when we discover that whisky is more than the sum of what we see, smell and taste. And, tasting is not confined to the characteristics of the whisky itself but encompasses the unique perceptions that individual tasters have, influenced by culture, prior experience, as well as current circumstances and expectations.

Circumstances may include weather, the company we are with, the mood we are in, or what we are eating or drinking at the time. To better understand and appreciate the experience, we begin with the aromatics and the origins of flavour that influence the character of the whisky.

Aromatics

Whisky contains hundreds of compounds that are influenced by the grain type, the malting and distilling process, the cask, and the length of time the whisky is aged. Tasting whisky involves a combination of sight, smell, taste and texture. Although separate senses, they are intimately entwined. The character and flavour of whisky is determined by how these flavour compounds have been married together. Examples of some of the flavour compounds found in whisky include phenols, aldehydes, lactones and esters.

Phenolic compounds, such as phenol, cresols, and guaiacols, contribute to the smokiness of some whiskies when barley is kiln dried using peat. Phenols and cresols provide the medicinal flavours while guaiacols are noted for smoky and woody flavours.

Aldehydes are produced during distillation and again appear from the oak when the whisky is being matured. The oak generates syringaldehydes that gives off a spicy, almond and vanilla taste, more commonly found in ex Bourbon barrels. During aging and maturing in casks, whisky is also influenced by the oak lactones in the wood that impart a coconut flavour.

Esters are emitted during the fermentation process from a combination of alcohol and fatty acids. Light esters emit a fruity or banana aroma. However, esters and fatty acids can be removed through chill filtration, which some believe does not affect the taste, even though logic may suggest otherwise.

Origins of Flavour in Whisky

The flavour of each whisky is dependent on many factors that range from how the barley is dried to the size and shape of the pot still. Other factors include the curvature and angle of the lyne arm, the length of time the whisky has matured in a cask, the type of cask used, and whether the cask is first fill or refill.

BARLEY

There are many types of barley used in Scotland. Examples of popular strains for making malt whisky are Belgravia, Concerto or Propino. Distillers look for barley that is low in nitrogen and high in starch with good enzyme potential for germination.

Malting barley is a process that involves steeping, germination and drying. When raw barley is steeped in water germination begins. Germination traditionally occurred on the malt floor after water was added, which takes about 3-5 days, and is then halted after 40-48 hours of kiln drying. Specialty malts are kiln dried at higher temperatures for longer periods to change the flavour of the malt. Varying the moisture level, time, and temperature of drying influences the flavour characteristics of each distinct malt.

PEAT

Depending on whether the kiln uses peat, gas or coal to dry the grain, flavours can range from peaty to light malty or subtle malt. Burning peat during the kilning process produces a smoky or 'peat reek' (smoke of a peat fire).

For distilleries that use peat to kiln dry the barley there are various types of peat from different areas of Scotland. Peat, itself, is a light brown to black organic sediment that is derived from the decomposition of mosses, grasses, heather shrubs and other wooded materials found in wet, boggy areas known as 'peatlands' or 'mires.' Sphagnum, the main component in peat, evokes a rubbery and old leathery boot smell, especially when burned.

Differences between peat compositions are based on climate, vegetation, bog type and cutting depth when harvesting. The peat used by the Scottish whisky industry is mainly from the north east of Scotland (Speyside and Aberdeenshire) and from the islands of Islay and Orkney.

Peatlands, throughout Scotland, are either blanket bogs or fens. Blanket bogs, such as those on Orkney, Speyside and Aberdeenshire, rely on heavy and consistent rainfall and low levels of evaporation and plant transpiration to remain waterlogged. Blanket bogs consist of sedges and grasses, with woody materials such as heather and other forested materials.

Fens, found in basins or valleys, are largely influenced by ground water from the surrounding soil. This peat has an abundance of sphagnum moss and contains less woody vegetation.

On the Isle of Islay there are both blanket bogs and fens that are used by the various distilleries. Castlehill is an example of a blanket bog that Port Ellen sources its peat from. Hobbister Hill (Highland Park), located on the Isle of Orkney, is also an example of a blanket bog, where sphagnum moss and other plants, such as sedges, heather and cotton grass are found.

Islay peat is rich in phenols, guaiacol, vanillin compounds and nitrogen, but contains less carbohydrate than the peat from the mainland. This is due to a greater amount of Sphagnum and lesser amount of wooden stemmed plants, such as heather, in Islay bogs.

Orkney peat contains more carbohydrate than Islay peats and more phenols than mainland peats from Tomintoul. The extraction depth is also important, especially on Orkney where there are great differences in peat composition. Surface peat on Orkney is closer to the mainland peat with the deeper layers resembling Islay peat.

Tomintoul in Speyside and St. Fergus in Aberdeenshire are basin bogs as well, but differ in chemical composition from the basin bogs on Islay. Both are rich in woody material. Arguably, this may have a lot to do with climate and microbiology than similar plant materials located in both sites.

In sum, the type of vegetation and level of decomposition and climatic conditions influence the chemical composition of peat. The flavour is also enhanced by the amount of time and smoke generated by the peat while in the kiln.

POT STILLS

Distillation is about alcohol vapours. How quickly the vapour forms, how much it rises, how much copper it touches, and how quickly it cools. Distillation begins by heating the wash in a copper pot (wash) still where the congeners are concentrated. The shape and size of the still determines the type of vapour interaction that occurs. Shorter pot stills deliver heavier, oily, waxier flavoured whisky, like Lagavulin or Macallan, and taller pot stills provide a more distinctive lighter whisky, such as Glenmorangie.

The copper in the still strips out some undesirable sulfurs from the distillate and the greater the surface area a still has the more the congeners - such as esters, phenols, and fusel alcohols - are removed from the vaporization stream.

Stills with more surface area, be they wider or taller than narrower stills, produce a less oily and more refined spirit.

LYNE ARM

The lyne arm is a cylindrical copper tube that connects the head (or neck) of the still to the condenser. When the vapours rise through the neck and into the lyne arm the temperature cools and the less volatile compounds, such as water and certain congeners, change from a gas into a liquid.

The lyne arm either angles upwards, runs horizontal or angles downwards. If ascending upwards, reflux is generated causing the spirit vapours to condense on the inside of the arm before draining back into the wash still. This will provide a lighter flavour and increase the alcohol content. If the lyne neck is angled down, this reduces the reflux and the heavy oils trickle into the condenser. This creates a heavier, more fulsome nutty spirit.

MATURATION

Most Scotch whisky distilleries use either Bourbon casks made of American white oak or Sherry casks made of either American white oak or European red oak. Both Bourbon and Sherry are used to either age/mature or finish the whisky, adding to the flavour profile.

Prior to use, Sherry, Madeira and Wine casks are toasted while Bourbon casks are charred. Or, alternatively, the cask may be shaved, toasted or re-charred. In both toasting and charring, the wood influences the flavour and character of the whisky during maturation.

The oak contains several compounds, such as hemicellulose, lignin, tannins, and oak lactones that diffuse into the spirit. These compounds lend flavour and colour, which after each use diminishes in intensity and consistency.

Hemicellulose, when exposed to high levels of heat, will caramelize leaving casks with notes of caramel, toffee or brown sugar. This is particularly true for Bourbon barrels that are charred, rather than toasted, prior to use.

Lignin, when combined with tannins, generates vanillan that leaves spice and vanilla expressions. Once again, the more the barrel is charred, the more the lignin yields flavour of smoke with notes of spice. The flavours we find in Bourbon casks include vanilla, honey, hazelnuts, fudge, ginger, butterscotch and coconut.

Tannins add astringency that leaves a pucker taste from the dryness it imparts. Tannins also remove unpleasant sulphur notes as the whisky ages in the cask, most notably in Sherry, wine and Madeira casks.

Oak lactones, sometimes referred to as whisky lactones, are responsible for the woody, coconut flavours also found in ex Bourbon casks. Lactones are formed during the toasting and charring of the casks giving the whisky its distinctiveness that range from vanilla or coconut to grass, sawdust to fruit-like flavour.

BOURBON CASKS

Bourbon casks came into use in Scotland following American prohibition and World War II. The Bourbon producers in the United States are only allowed to use these oak barrels once. This was due to the successful lobbying of the American Coopers Union to keep their members employed. (The cooperage industry collapsed during Prohibition).

The white oak was best-suited for making watertight barrels used for shipping (or more accurately floating) the Kentucky Bourbon down the Mississippi River to the East Coast. Single use barrels created an abundant supply and provided an inexpensive source of barrels for the Scotch whisky industry. Today, Bourbon barrels make up about 90 percent of the casks used to make whisky in Scotland.

Bourbon casks, unlike Sherry, wine and Madeira casks, are charred on the inside before they are used. Charring creates a carbon filter that helps to mitigate the sharp and intense compounds, such as sulphur that occur during distillation.

Although most whiskies are initially aged in Bourbon barrels, many are now finished with ex-Sherry or, more recently, with Caribbean rum, different wines, Indian Pale Ale, and Canadian Ice Wine.

Examples of 'pure' ex-Bourbon matured whiskies are Bowmore, Tullibardine Sovereign, Glenfiddich 19-year Bourbon Cask Reserve, Ardbeg 10-year., Glenmorangie 10-year, Glenlivet 12-year, and Laphroaig Quarter Cask.

SHERRY CASKS

Sherry casks (or butts) were introduced to Scotland in large volume following the phloxera aphid infestation that destroyed the wine industry in France in the mid-1800s. The English, who were large importers of wine and Cognac, switched to Sherry as an alternative. Sherry was imported in 'transport' casks and bottled in London. Rather than being sent back to Spain, these casks were sold to Highland (and Island) distilleries and were used to mature young spirit, giving the whisky a new flavour expression. This made single malt more palatable that helped spur the first whisky boom in the late 1800s. However, since 1981, bulk exports of Sherry casks have been banned, which means that the Scottish whisky industry has their Sherry casks made exclusively for their needs. Today, rather than a re-used cask, a new oak cask is prepared using either American or European oak and sent to a Sherry bodega to be filled with a seasoning wine to round off the edges.

Most Sherry, Madeira and wine casks are toasted rather than charred. Toasting mellows the tannins and releases vanillin from the cellulose in the wood. The less toasting, the less vanillin and caramel notes. Like charring, there are varying degrees of toasting from light to heavy leaving the cask with stronger and more distinctive flavours.

For whisky aged in Sherry casks, first fill Pedro Ximenes is the sweetest, with toffee, fruit and molasses notes. Oloroso is less sweet, with walnut and fruitcake expressions. And, Fino Sherry is a dry Sherry with earthy, almond-like flavours. Other taste profiles for Sherry include dried fruits, nutmeg, orange, candied peel and Christmas cake.

Nose: Connecting Smell to Memory

The process of nosing the whisky starts with the vaporized odor molecules drawn in through the nostrils and embedded in the mucus lining the roof of the nose. This is where the olfactory epithelium is located with its specialized olfactory receptor neurons that detect the aromas in whisky.

These receptor neurons connect to the olfactory bulb located at the back of the nose that processes sensory input, linking the brain and limbic system where emotions and memories are activated. As it perceives certain odors, the limbic system accesses experiences that remind us about people, places and events stored in our memory. Most of what is recognized through this process is instinctive rather than produced through conscious thought.

The scent bearing molecules (congeners) found in whisky not only help us distinguish one whisky from another, but create the possibility of triggering a previous experience, such as a childhood memory that may lead to a certain emotion that plays on the senses in the moment.

Palate: Intersection of Smell, Taste and Texture

When whisky is tasted, these aromatic compounds, detected through the nostrils, now cross the threshold of our taste buds lining the tongue, releasing more aromas. These cells detect sweet, sour, salt, bitter, fatty, and umami. We previously learned that sweetness is noted by receptors on the tip of the tongue, while saltiness and acidity are noted on the sides, with bitterness located at the back of the tongue. However, we have since learned that this is a myth and that tastes are sensed across the tongue.

Texture, on the other hand, provides a sensuousness in the mouth that can range from a soft and velvety to creamy and oily, waxy or even prickly with some cask strength whiskies. Astringent mouthfeel, such as dryness, furriness or a powdery texture, are most noticeable when we swallow.

What we smell and taste is subjective. The language is descriptive and the process for discovering this amazing sensory experience is imaginative and recollective.

Appearance does play a part when we observe color, clarity or viscosity, but we contend that since colour has been altered by E150a for many distilleries (albeit now less so due to public concern), but regardless of what the hue might be there is no correlation between colour with smell or taste.

> *In October 2011, a vial of unmatured malt from the Ardbeg Distillery on Islay was sent to the International Space Station in a cargo spacecraft, along with some charred oak. Another vial of the same whisky was kept at the distillery for comparison on its return. Scientists are now comparing how the chemicals interacted and flavours materialized at close-to-zero gravity.*

SEVEN

LANGUAGE OF WHISKY

Back in 1979, a group of sensory analysts devised a language of whisky at the Pentlands Scotch Whisky Research Institute, now known as the Scotch Whisky Research Institute (SWRI) in Edinburgh. The SWRI is a consortium of independent distillers whose purpose is to provide expertise in non-engineering aspects of Scotch whisky production. In doing so, they developed a tasting wheel diagram which has become the industry standard and since that time numerous iterations of the wheel (and other similar schematics) have emerged.

Whisky writers found a common language, using certain words to characterize different tastes. For instance, whiskies were categorized as "smoky", "rich", "light" and "delicate" and within these categories more detailed descriptors were used, such as woody, herbal, buttery, nutty, toffy, leather, cereal, citrusy, peppery, iodine, spicy and so on.

Sensory differentiation was intended to make sense of the complex range of smell and taste, using science to analyze the data and then marketing to help promote the brands. This has become the language of 'tasting notes' found on whisky containers (and some bottles), as well as a myriad of websites.

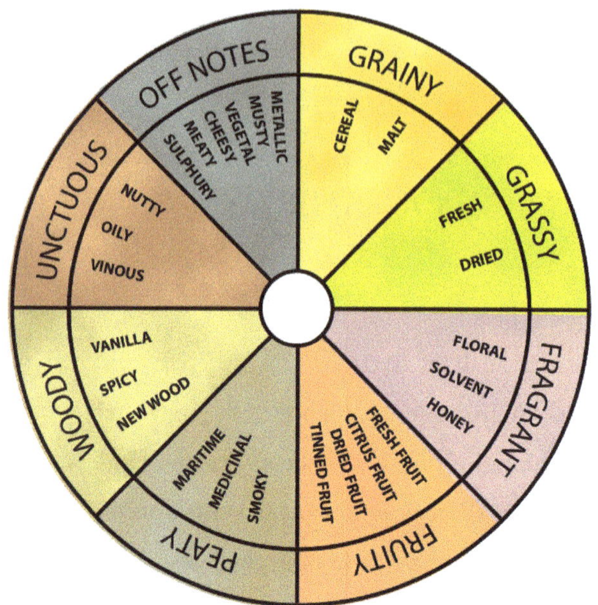

Figure 14 Charles Maclean Whisky Wheel

Charles MacLean, a widely published authority on Scotch whisky, trained in 'the sensory evaluation of potable spirits' at the Scotch Whisky Research Institute, has compiled a list of descriptors that denotes sensory differentiation. In his book *Whiskypedia: A Gazetteer of Scotch Whisky* (2014), he provides insight into how language is used in describing categories of aroma commonly found in whisky.

GRAINY

Cereal - breakfast cereal, porridge, grits, bran, toast, digestive biscuits, coffee

Malt - malted milk, malt barn, Horlicks, Marmite

GRASSY

Fresh - cut grass, green vegetables, green sticks, tomato, leafy, mint

Dried - hay, straw, chaff, dried tea, stewed tea, tobacco, dried herbs

FRAGRANT

Floral - scented, perfumed, blossom, lavender, wall-flower, geranium, artificial floral

Solvent - bubble gum, pear drops, fresh paint, acetone, cellophane, pine essence

Honey - clover flowers, heather pollen, spun honey, acacia honey, mead, beeswax

FRUITY

Fresh Fruit - apple, pear, peach, melon, fresh fig, cherry, raspberry, banana, red current

Citrus Fruit - lemon, lime, orange, mandarin, grapefruit, pineapple

Dried Fruit - raisins, sultanas, figs, mince pies, Christmas cake, marmalade

Tinned Fruit - peaches, pears, fruit salad, lychees, mandarin

WOODY

New Wood - sap, resin, sawdust, pencil shavings, cigar boxes, sandalwood

Vanilla - ice cream, custard, caramel, fudge, toffee, crystalline sugar, syrup, crème brulee

Spicy – clove, nutmeg, cinnamon, aniseed, liquorice, ginger, chilli, black pepper, garam masala, coffee grounds

UNCTUOUS

Vinous - white wine, Sherry, Madeira, red wine, port, brandy, wine cellar

Oily - cream, butter, vegetable oil, chocolate, olive, candlewax, soap

Nutty - coconut, nut oil, linseed oil, almond, walnut, hazelnut

OFF-NOTES

Sulphury - starch, linen, rubber, struck matches, cordite, spent fireworks, exhaust fumes

Meaty - leather, cowhide, boiled pork, sausages, roast meat, gravy

Cheesy - cheese, rancid butter, fat, goaty, mousey, yeasty, sweaty, baby vomit

Vegetal - brackish, stale, cabbage water, cooked swede, ketchup, vinegar, marsh gas, bogs

Musty - earthy, fusty, mossy, mouldy, corked, damp wool, mothballs

Metallic - inky, tinny, wet iron, rusty

PEATY

Smoky - lapsang souchong tea, peat smoke, smoked salmon, kippers, tar, creosote

Medicinal - sphagnum moss, lint, Elastoplast, hospitals, dentists

Maritime - brine, seaweed, shellfish, fresh fish.

Tasting Notes

The language of whisky tasting notes can be helpful. However, some appear as short outbursts of undulating prose. For example, the most distinctive aroma and taste in single malt Scotch is from the peat. "Peaty" describes whiskies that range from a "medicinal', "smoky" (or sometimes both), with hints of iodine, ash tray or a leathery old boot. Some peat aroma may have a salty, maritime scent, while other peaty whiskies may effuse spicy or heathery notes instead.

The peat on Islay, for example, has its own distinctive taste and smell. Whiskies from distilleries such as Ardbeg, Lagavulin, Laphroaig and Bruichladdich with their Octomore series are especially known for their distinct peaty, sometimes smoky or combination of the two. David Broom suggests Lagavulin 16 year isn't 'smoky', but rather "its peat moves into a weird territory of Lapsang Souchong tea and pipe tobacco, fishboxes and kippers." Whereas others have described Ardbeg – Uigeadail as a "…beguiling mix of warm Christmas cake and walnut oil fused with fresh ocean spice…followed by a smoky coal fire and a deep scent of well-oiled leather".

By comparison, the peat on the Isle of Orkney, Skye and Mull have a heathery base and is less medicinal in taste, offering a salty and bitter character instead. A Highland Park 12 year from Isle of Orkney is noted as having a "hint of heathery smoke and charcoal…some grassy notes, hay, mingling nicely with the soft smoky touches". Or, the Ledaig 10-year-old from the Tobermory Distillery on the Isle of Mull, has been described as "very tarry and ash with lots of tobacco notes up front…a lot of wet wool…anchovies in salt…intense sooty notes".

Single malts from the Highlands and Speyside regions, on the other hand, are considered lighter and more delicate. This is not to suggest that all Highland or Speyside whiskies are lighter or delicate as some are drying their malts with peat, while others are experimenting with different casks to enhance the whisky tasting experience. It is only to say that the tasting note descriptions can be less colourful.

Glenfiddich, for instance, introduced their new IPA Experiment that is finished by aging it for three months in reused IPA (Indian Pale Ale) casks, leaving it with "lots of fruit, some cinnamon, grassy and a bit hoppy". Or, Glenfiddich's Winter Storm Ice Wine Casks 21 year, aged in Canadian ice wine barrels from Peller Estate Winery in Ontario, has been described as "quite tangy …followed by something biscuity, most reminiscent of cookie dough, and a hint of desiccated coconut." Some might consider this more tantalizing than tasting an old leather boot, while licking a turn of the century ashtray.

Tasting Notes Unravelled

Tasting notes are now an integral part of the marketing of single malts. Distiller notes are often found on the container or on their website. Other popular tasting notes sites are found in online websites - Masters of Malt and Whisky Exchange as two of many examples. The challenge for the whisky explorer is when tasting notes of the same whisky varies from one author description to another. For example:

Glenmorangie Quinta Ruban Port Cask Finish 12 year

NOSE: *Distiller Notes* - Dark mint chocolate, tangerines and Seville oranges mingle with sandalwood and walnut before giving way to a spicy finish of pepper and nutmeg.

NOSE: *Chaps at Masters of Malt* - Full of winter berries and a touch of port. A good oak and a little cereal hanging in the substratum.

> PALATE: *Distiller Notes* - Mint chocolate and walnuts envelop the palate like velvet, laying the foundations for rose, Turkish delight and sweet Seville oranges.
>
> PALATE: *Chaps at Master of Malt* - Sweet and thick. The port note is chewy and rich with notes of barley sugar and cereal and lots of juicy fruit and berries, a tad cloying.

FINISH: *Distiller Notes* - Long lasting silky aftertaste leaving dark chocolate mints and traces of orange.

FINISH: *Chaps at Master of Malt* - Long and fruity and quite sweet.

Aberlour A'Bunadh Batch 55

NOSE: *Distiller Notes* - Aromas of mixed spices, praline and spiced orange harmonising with rich, deep notes of Oloroso Sherry.

NOSE: *Chaps at Master of Malt* - Heavily sherried malt, walnuts, dark chocolate and clove.

> PALATE: *Distiller Notes* - Orange, black cherries, dried fruit and ginger spiked with dark bitter chocolate and enriched with Sherry and Oak. Full bodied and creamy.

> PALATE: *Chaps at Master of Malt* - Sweeter and fruitier on the palate, with bags of orange segments and black cherries developing against the intense Christmas spices.

FINISH: *Distiller Notes* - Robust and intense with bitter-sweet notes of exotic spices, dark chocolate and oak.

FINISH: *Chaps at Master of Malt* - A little bit of damp tobacco lingers alongside mocha and sweet Sherry.

Laphroaig Quarter Cask

NOSE: *Whisky Exchange* - Powerful smoke, sweet malt, wet turf, coal. Develops chocolate & cinnamon.

NOSE: *Chaps at Masters of Malt* - Oily and buttery nose, with toffee, nuttiness, hickory, bicarbonate of soda, rum and raisin ice cream and zest.

> PALATE: *Whisky Exchange* - Full-bodied, rich and mouth-coating. Delicious sweet gristy malt and rich peat, woodsmoke. The coal appears mid-palate.

PALATE: *Chaps at Master of Malt* - Big rush of sweetness, in fact it's an explosion of sweetness, with fiery chilli heat, TCP, sweet cereals and a touch of cola syrup.

FINISH: *Whisky Exchange* - Very long, sweet and smoky, with the coal lingering longest.

FINISH: *Chaps at Master of Malt* - Medium-length, but becomes fruity, with custard and cigar smoke.

In short, you might wonder if they were nosing and tasting the same single malt, as each has discovered and described something different from the other. What you can take from this is that nosing, and tasting is personal and subjective. Although tasting notes are helpful for the whisky explorer, the key is personal discovery rather than authored descriptions.

Charles Maclean, in his book Whiskypedia: A Gazetteer of Scotch Whisky, says that appreciating the experience of a dram "…engages all of our senses – sight, smell, taste, touch (i.e. texture), even, some would say hearing." Further, he notes that our noses are the "ultimate arbiters of quality in whisky", while tasting notes are simply entertaining and appetizing.

> *At its best, the language used to describe the aroma and flavour of whisky is both colorful and objective; at worst it is marketing hyperbole, bearing little relationship to the product described.*

EIGHT

PAIRING WITH FOOD

Pairing is about connecting something with something else or someone with someone else. The key to pairing is discovering what makes the pairing work.

For instance, pairing what you drink with what you eat is not a new phenomenon, especially when it comes to pairing food and wine. With a good Pinot Noir, Pinot Gris, Riesling or Cabernet Sauvignon the range of food choice is limitless. The question is what foods (if any) pair with a single malt and which single malts in particular?

Figure 15 Three Chimney's Restaurant, Isle of Skye

What we learned is that when it comes to single malt whisky there are some foods that complement the peaty, smoky malts and there are other foods that are better suited with rich and floral or lighter malts. And, we learned that there are some foods or spices that you may want to avoid altogether. These include foods that have a lot of garlic or onions or are very spicy or bitter tasting that mask whisky flavours on the palate. For example, peaty and smoky malts paired with smoky foods, such as smoked salmon, neutralize the delicate flavours of both the food and the whisky, which loses the essence of both. Pairing smoked salmon with a lighter floral whisky works very well because the smokiness of the salmon is not lost.

A Sherry cask whisky, such as a Glendronach or a Macallan pairs well with more heavily flavoured dishes, such as lamb, pork or beef. BBQ steak works well with most malts, but steaks that are charred provide a special delight with a peaty whisky like a Bowmore, Laphroaig, Lagavulin or Ardbeg.

When it comes to cheese, Brie works well with the earthy, maritime and brine tones of Talisker or an Old Pulteney. Others like their blue cheese with peaty Islay malts. Camembert, Gouda or Havarti blend well with Royal Lochnagar (Highland), Dalwhinnie (Highland) or Glenfiddich, Glenlivet or Cardhu (Speyside).

CHOCOLATE

Chocolate is especially noteworthy when it comes to whisky pairing. The darker the chocolate (70% + cocoa content) the more the smoky, peaty whiskies take the tasting experience to another level. The peat and smoke, on the other hand, doesn't seem to work nearly as well with sweeter milk chocolate, which we discovered was much better served with lighter, floral tastes.

Notwithstanding, some chocoholics don't care what they drink, as they will eat whatever chocolate passes their lips and savour it with whatever happens to be in the glass or cup at the time.

Figure 16 Wendy's Whisky Fudge

At home, Wendy made a deep chocolate whisky fudge with Dalmore 12 year and another with Laphroaig Quarter Cask, using a combination of dark (Callebaut) chocolate, with a bit of semi-sweet added.

She then tried *Talisker Storm*, increasing the combination of dark with semi-sweet, but this time topped with coarse sea salt, which turned out to be a real favourite. If it is possible to let the fudge sit for a week or two, without losing your mind while you wait – this gives some time for the whisky and the chocolate to marry. Nothing more to be said…

SALMON MARINATED IN SINGLE MALT

For those who enjoy their salmon, marinating salmon with two tablespoons of your favourite single malt is a delicious way to experiment with whisky and food pairing. In our case, we used Singleton Single Malt Whisky of Dufftown Tail Fire, with its notes of pealed oak, walnut husks and cut grass – mixed in with two tablespoons of maple syrup and one tablespoon of Maillie Dijon mustard and then letting it sit overnight. When ready to grill, adding grated lemon and lemon juice and barbequing on soaked cedar plank for about 20 minutes at medium heat. Finishing the dish with pan-fried prawns, wild rice and a spinach salad. And, savouring the dish with a dram of Cardhu 12 year adding its own oak and sweet malt evoking flavours.

For those seeking more adventure, you could easily peat it up with an Ardbeg, Laphroaig or Lagavulin to give it that campfire smoke, charcoal and woodsy expression to offset the sweetness of the maple syrup.

OYSTERS & AN ISLAY DRAM

Oysters on the west coast of British Columbia are divine. Examples include Buckley Bay beach grown oysters on Denman Island, the sweet and salty Fanny Bay oysters off the east coast of Vancouver Island or Little Wing and Okeover Organic oysters from Okeover Inlet at the south end of Desolation Sound near Lund. The brine of the oyster, while still in its shell, complements well the maritime and peaty tastes of Islay whiskies, as well as some lighter, fragrant whiskies. After tasting each on its own, pour the whisky over the oyster and eat it from the shell.

WHISKY TASTING & FOOD PAIRING

In our exploration to learn more about food and whisky pairing, Blue Collar and Scholar hosted a series of whisky tasting and pairing events with Chef John D. Walls from Culinary Magic and the Modern Peasant Restaurant in Powell River.

Like whisky, there are fruity esters, spicy phenolics and sulphur containing molecules in food. The key is to find the right combination to pair with each of the whiskies served. The other key to pairing is to find the right progression of tastes and mouthfeel. For instance, progressing from a lighter floral whisky to a peatier one works better than the other way around. Similarly with food, the progression of tastes is also important to pair with the right combination.

Starting with Auchentoshan Triple Wood, Chef Walls prepared a roasted radish salad with grilled asparagus to start things off. The radish was subtle to the taste but when combined with the asparagus was playful with the Auchentoshan enhancing the fresh fruit and oaky flavours of the whisky.

With a Glendronach Original Sherry Casks 12-year-old, he offered pan seared duck breast with an onion jam, Sherry reduction and Spruce infused oil over a Scottish bannock. Here, he paired the sweet and nuttiness of the Sherry reduction with the with the fruity, black pepper notes from the Spanish Pedro Ximenez and Oloroso sherry of the whisky. A dry and nutty, slightly spicy finish of the whisky combined with the duck left a longer sweeter finish than expected.

Figure 17 Chef John D. Walls

Highland Park Full Volume was paired with wild oyster and morel mushroom Ragu. To add to the savory smell, he adorned the bowl with a small handful of moss gathered from the local forest and with it he provided a quick shot of steam to the moss. This combination of light smoke, pineapple and honey vanilla of the Highland Park with the sweet mysterious forested odors of the moss infused with the dirt, rainy, earthy mushroom smell, truly piqued the sensory receptors in the nose. Clearly, a favorite!

For the last dish he served vanilla cream butterflied prawns covered with pearly barley and steamed green onions with Ardbeg Uigeadail. With a caramel infused smoke and a touch of leather boot on the nose, this provided a beautiful introduction to a mix of the whisky's oily mouthfeel and the sweet vanilla cream of the prawns, leaving a combination of spicy sweet and smoky barley taste with plenty of texture. And, with it, a long finish that left one sitting stunned, waiting for more.

All these dishes were offered as tastings, served without wine. There are more and more chefs exploring food tastings with single malt. Michelin chefs, like Eric Pras, have been known to substitute whisky for wine at gatherings (Aberlour's Saint-Hubert festival). While other Michelin star chefs, such as the Rocco brothers from the El Celler de Can Roca in Girona, Spain (world's best restaurant 2017) has partnered with Macallan and Chef Massimo Bottura from Osteria Francescana in Modena, Italy (world's best restaurant in 2018) has partnered with Dalmore.

The seasoned whisky aficionados have marvelled at how well the different choices of whiskies worked with different foods. And, for those who were new to the 'water of life' and considered themselves largely wine devotees or beer drinkers also marvelled at what they discovered through nosing and tasting and through mouthfeel as well. Whether an aficionado or neophyte, sharing their discoveries with others made the pairing experience a highlight when combined with a little history, science and lore.

The key to tasting and food pairing is experimenting, either on your own or in a group. We know some foods and whiskies pair very well and some less so. Here are some examples of pairing choices that have been enjoyed by many we have talked to:

LIGHT FRAGRANT WHISKIES WITH A TOUCH OF FLORAL SWEETNESS

Glenfiddich 12 year, Glenlivet Nadurra Oloroso Cask, Auchentoshan, Royal Lochnagar, Dalwhinnie, Glenkinchie 12 year, Cardhu 18 year, Knockando 12, 15,

& 18-year, Flora & Fauna Collection (Auchroisk, Glen Spey, Glenlossie, Inchgower, Strathmill, Teaninich)

Sushi and sashimi

Smoked salmon

Wild salmon

Sturgeon

Crab, scallops and prawns

Camembert, Gouda, Havarti, Brie

Raw Oysters

Indian and Thai curries

Fresh fruits

MEDIUM BODIED WHISKIES WITH SOME PEAT

Bruichladdich Laddie 10 year, Cardhu 12 year, Bunnahabhain, Highland Park Viking Series, Old Pulteney 12 year, Clynelish, Tomintoul, Aberlour

Grilled chicken and steak

Goat cheese

Seared scallops and bacon

Smoked mussels and oyster

Smoked duck and venison

Mushrooms

FULL-BODIED WHISKIES AGED IN SHERRY CASKS

Aberlour A'Bunadh and 12 years Sherry Cask Matured, Ardbeg Uigeadail, The Macallan Double Cask 12 year, Highland Park 18 year and Dark Origins, Glendronach 12 year Original, Dalmore 15 year, Tomatin 18 year, Tamdhu Batch

Strength, The Balvenie 15 Year, Bowmore 15 year, Kilchoman Loch Gorm, Glenfarclas 17 year

Seared or grilled steak

Christmas pudding

Pecan pie

Sticky toffee pudding

Roast venison

Gingerbread or ginger cookies

Dark chocolate brownies

Matured cheddar

Dried fruit and unsalted nuts

STRONG, PEATED WHISKIES

Lagavulin 12 & 16 years, Ardbeg 10 years, Talisker 10 years and Talisker Storm, Laphroaig Cairdeas Quarter Cask, Bruichladdich Octomore Masterclass 8.3 edition.

Salmon, Halibut, Sturgeon or Cod

Oysters – raw or steamed (pouring it into the shell)

Haggis

Ham and salami

Brie

Apple wood smoked cheddar

Strong blue cheeses – Roquefort, Stilton, Gorgonzola

Apple crumble

Chocolate with high cocoa content (70% or higher)

Dried fruit and heavily roasted nuts

NINE

PAIRING WITH CIGARS

Being reflective means sitting in a comfortable chair, peering out into the rain and fog with a cigar and a dram. Exposed to the elements, on the other hand, is being outside with a dram and a slightly wet cigar, wondering if you are wet enough to go in.

A light sweet or fruity malt, like a Glenkinchie or a Glenmorangie, is amazing when the fog is rolling in and the rain has not yet materialized. And when it does, a rich and maritime malt like Talsiker Storm adds texture and deep pondering as the rain intensifies. And, when the fog is deep and foreboding, a Lagavulin, Laphroaig or Ardbeg settles the spirit and prepares the mind for more to come.

Figure 18 Dalmore Cigar Malt+Cohiba

Cigar pairing with whisky has had a long history of smoke-filled bars or cigar lounges festooned with large stuffed vintage leather club chairs. Although the cigar lounge has been replaced by anti-smoking sentiment, the image has prevailed among a new generation of whisky explorers.

The range of cigars is unlimited. There are certain types of cigars though that pair much easier with a light fragrant whisky, rather than a full body or a strong peaty dram. Like food, the key to determining the right complement is through individual experimentation.

What might not work for one, may still please another, given a myriad of circumstances, mood and temperament at the time.

What we learned is that a highly peated whisky does not match well with a light and mild cigar, such as a Romeo Y Juliet, as the smoky, peaty taste will overwhelm the lightness of the cigar. A better choice is pairing a Romeo with a Highland or Speyside malt. George Koutsakis, a drinks and spirits writer for Forbes and Food and Wine magazines, suggests it's about finding your balance.

Whiskies with notes of vanilla and caramel combine nicely with lighter sweeter cigars. For instance, Maduro aged cigars pair well with Highland malts such as Old Pulteney, Glenmorangie, Clynelish and with Speyside malts such as The Balvenie, Glenfiddich and The Glenlivet.

Dalmore has taken the cigar pairing to another level with its Dalmore Cigar Malt Reserve. Pairing the Dalmore with a Partagas Serie D No 4, was recommended by Dalmore and James J. Fox at a 2017 seminar at the London Whisky Show. This pairing combines Dalmore's notes of honey and cigar smoke with its earthy toniness.

For one of our experiments, we paired a CAO Mx2 Dagger cigar with an Ardbeg 10 year. What was exciting about the combination was that the cigar brought out a sweetness in the smoke and peat of the Ardbeg that neither of us had recognized before. We were like two kids hammering on as if we were finding tadpoles in an old crusty pond.

A pairing to try is one of the Cohiba Siglo series, with its mild creamy bean-like flavour, with a Glenlivet 12 year with its caramel, malt and vanilla. Another is Glenfiddich 21-year Reserva Rum Cask with a Romeo Y Julieta Exhibicion No. 4.

This combines the sweet banana and caramel of the rum cask with the dark chocolate and leathery spice of the cigar.

So, for those who enjoy a good cigar, the key is to discover the dance of the smoke with the right single malt. What influences the taste and balance is a combination of factors that range from mood, weather, romantic interests (which can work for or against enjoying a good cigar) or being philosophically aligned to certain planets and star clusters at the right moment. And yes, cigar pairing is not for everyone and may require a night on the couch - knowing that the right pairing is worth the reward.

> *The choice of cigar and dram should inspire and not distract. Whatever the choice, nosing the spirit of the whisky as it infuses with the spiraling smoke of a cigar brings a sense of pleasure to the moment when the whisky crosses the threshold of the palate - as if in a dream.*

Figure 19

It was late in the summer season and eagle down rained from cedar trees without the work of wind or beating wing, a September ripe with paradox. I was working as a guide in Haida Gwai and staying at the Hodge-Podge Lodge, where I recall the 'Old Boy' presenting me with a ruffled and pleated, lemon yellow, 1970's tuxedo that I was to wear to a special event that evening. It fit 'to a T' so I did not rally against the expectation! Later that evening I recall being baited by another guide, along with a dram or two of Lagavulin 16 year that enlightened my palate, to wear my newly acquired yellow tuxedo through the Vancouver International Airport during my air travels home and if I complied, I would be awarded one bottle of the same. As it were, this became my first take-away bottle of the Water of Life

Figure 20

TEN

PAIRING WITH ACTIVITES

Figure 21 Blue Collar tossing the caber

When it comes to the Scottish Highland Games Heavy Events, what could be better than pairing Scotch with a great caber throw (presumably after the toss)? Man, against stone, steel and wood has deep historical roots in Scotland. The heavy events games were a way of choosing the most able of men for the clan chieftain's household. The events were also used for military training and with the addition of the pipers and dancers brought more fanfare and prestige to the participating clans.

The thrill of the competition, the comradery amongst competitors and the celebration and reward of hard work and perseverance in preparation for the day's events, all help at the end of the day make a dram (or three) of Bruichladdich Octomore Masterclass 8.3 edition taste divine. The Octomore with its 309.1PPM (Phenol Parts per Million) is like being at the top of your game.

As an automotive service technician. I diagnose and repair cars for 10 hours a day. Then, for an average of 2 hours a day, I train for the coming Scottish Heavy Events season or coach Track and Field and sometimes both. At the end of the day I am physically and mentally exhausted. To be able to do all this on top of being a devoted father and husband, I need to recover. My favourite way to recover, both physically and mentally, is a relaxing soak in our hot tub. As soon as I submerge into the heat of the water, all my aches and pains and stiffness begin to melt away. That instant wave of relaxation helps to clear the mind as well. With no electronic distractions and a dram of cask strength Tobermory 9-year-old this helps make a perfect malt and mind free moment.

The Beach

The sun is warm, the air crisp and full of salt spray. The tidal surge is crashing, and with each epic wave the foam comes just inches from the tops of our gumboots. We walk quiet and peaceful with our eyes watching for treasures in the sea debris, deposited along the stretches of open sand… while we keep a wary eye out for the rogue wave determined to catch us off guard.

Smiling, returning to the warmth of our cabin, our gait just a little quicker knowing that there will be a sweet promise on arrival. Gumboots kicked off, toques and mitts discarded, there waiting are sweet dark and salty caramel chocolates along with the golden glow of a slightly peaty Scotch whisky, in this case Bunnahabhain 12 year.

A warm sunlit memory; sweet, salty chocolate and the golden glow of Bunnahabhain… a pairing made in heaven.

ELEVEN

PAIRING WITH SUNSETS

There is nothing more satisfying at the end of a day than watching the sun set holding a dram of choice in view as the sun descends into the evening horizon. Alone, there can be a sense of contentment as we watch the colours fuse into a multitude of hues. With a lover, it becomes a statement of playfulness and celebration. So, raising a glass of Glen Garioch 12 year, for example, with its slight orange peel and vanilla sweetness, finishes nicely with a whiff of salty air and a caramel sky.

Figure 22 Lund, British Columbia

Figure 23 Salish Sea

The restless spirit of the mind, captured by the last vestiges of the sun, pairs well with the welcoming spirit of a dram taking us to a place of momentary reverence.

TWELVE

E-VALUATING FOR THE FUTURE

The Scotch Whisky Association in their 2018 report said that a new generation of whisky industry entrepreneurs was emerging; and the modern consumer demographic was shifting from North American and European markets to Asian markets. New Asian whiskies were capturing the limelight, with India now leading the top 30 whisky sales in the world by volume. These include Officers Choice, McDowell's No.1, Imperial Blue and Royal Stag, with Johnny Walker and Jack Daniel's following behind.

For the single malts, Asian whiskies of note are those produced in Japan, such as Hakushu, Kakubin and Black Nikka Clear and in Taiwan, Kavalan is taking whisky aficionados by storm. Elsewhere, there has been strong growth in volume of Scotch exports to Latvia, Russia, China, and South Africa.

The world's best-selling single malt Scotch continues to be Glenfiddich; The Glenlivet, the best-selling single malt in the UK; and Glenmorangie Original, the best-selling single malt in Scotland. Macallan dominates the rare whisky scene and is now one of the top four best-selling Scotch single malts in the world.

In search of new markets, some Scottish whisky producers are pushing back on long standing practices of stating the age of the whisky and introducing instead 'non-age statement' brands as if hiding their youthfulness.

Producers are also experimenting with different refill casks that range from beer to ice wine. And, independent bottlers are seeding further experimentation and innovation in defining their place in the global market. However, as Dave Broom noted in his August 2018 ScotchWhisky.com article, "[t]rying to be all things to all drinkers isn't the answer". Experimentation and innovation may be important strategic tools, but innovation, in and of itself, can be a "blind alley" if it lacks a connection to the whisky consumer. Although blended Scotch makes up ninety percent of the global Scotch whisky market with its blend of grains and malt, we believe that single malt Scotch represents the essence of what the whisky distilling industry is all about. Reflected in its legacy is its long standing tradition, which includes its individuality, integrity and authenticness.

Tradition is about the distilling process and the methods and practices that have been maintained over the past two hundred plus years. Although there have been numerous changes since the days when each distillery grew its own barley and had its own malting floor, new technology was introduced to help meet a growing demand. Consistency and quality of the whisky is what remains central.

Individuality, for industry, often means product differentiation. But for the consumer/explorer individuality means connecting whisky choice to identity or lifestyle expression, regardless of whether they are a millennial or baby boomer. And, with more and more distilleries producing new products and with it more marketing hyperbole, the consumer/explorer can be easily overwhelmed.

Seeking ways to educate the public is always a good place to start. Unfortunately, there is a barrage of misinformation that feeds the current market. Knowing that not all Scotch is smoky, there is no single flavour profile for each whisky region, and that the age of whisky cannot be determined by its colour helps mitigate some of the misinformation.

The question is whose responsibility is it to ensure the information is correct? Is it the whisky producers, the media or does the responsibility rest with whisky proponents - be they brand ambassadors, bartenders or online 'experts' - to know the difference between fact and myth? We contend that each has a part to play. The whisky proponents are the face or front line of the industry and any misinformation they impart simply adds to customer confusion. Educating those who work in the industry is a must.

The whisky distillers and independent bottling producers also have a responsibility to ensure branding information is accurate and the narratives they tell represents the values of the distillery, its history and location. Many distillers are applying short impact narratives, using history, environment and legacy as part of the allure of the label. In reviewing distillery websites, clearly some distillers are demonstrating how useful a good story or narrative can be.

Isle of Orkney

Highland Park's uses the slogan "standing apart not standing alone". They have built a story line for its whiskies around its Viking ancestry. Starting in 2012, Highland Park unleashed Thor – the Norse god of thunder and lightning – followed by Loki, Freya and Odin. Today's Highland Park describes itself as an Orkney single malt with a Viking soul. Their 10-year-old is Viking Scars, their 12-year-old is referred to as Viking Honour, and their 18-year-old is Viking Pride.

The Scapa distillery, on the other hand, focuses on the 'island, elements and weather'. Their 'claim to fame' is that they are the only distillery in Scotland to use a Lomond still to create their whisky. (The Lomond still, introduced in the 1950s by Hiram Walker, allows distillers to make a range of whisky styles and create different flavour profiles for blending.) While one distillery boldly claims its heritage the other blends gently into the environment.

Isle of Islay

Islay distilleries emphasize both their location and flavour expressions that include iodine, seaweed and salt to differentiate themselves from other peated whiskies. Like other distilleries, Islay distilleries differentiate their product lines through compelling narratives.

For Bunnahabhain and Bowmore their story is about their history. For Laphroaig, it is about friendship - "We don't make friends easily, but when we do, they're for life." Their marketing approach is to offer a "honorary lifetime lease on a plot of land (an entire square foot)" on Islay.

Ardbeg has created Ardbeg Embassies and Outposts throughout the world and, as well, an Ardbeg Committee "with a worldwide membership of over 120,000 and counting".

Bruichladdich, on the other hand, having recently re-emerged from mothballing, differentiates itself from other Islay distilleries by being the 'outlier'. Their innovation was to create the peatiest whisky of all with their introduction of the Octomore series. As well, they have introduced the first gin on the island and saturated their product line with thirty-five releases. As they say on their website, "We respect the past but don't live in its shadow. We believe in innovation and progress, while striving to create intriguing spirit – a spirit with flawless integrity and provenance. We are curious and restless – never leave well enough alone."

Speyside

Glenfiddich's branding message is 'collaboration' in finding new expressions in their experimental cask series. In 2016, they introduced IPA (Indian Pale Ale) cask finish, which was followed by Project XX, where they invited 20 industry experts to create a new offering. The third in the experimental series is their Winter Storm using Ice Wine casks from Peller Estates at Niagara-on-the-Lake in Canada to cask finish.

The Macallan takes a more conservative approach "where innovation meets tradition" and links their whisky to the culinary wizardry of the Roca brothers from El Celler de Can Roca restaurant in Girona, Spain. For the Macallan, this links them to what they call the 'sources of excellence'.

Highlands

The Dalmore brand identity is based on a legend dating back to the 13th Century with the story of a young man named Colin of Kintail who saves King Alexander III from a charging stag. For his bravery he was awarded the lands of Eilean Donan and the right to bear the 12-pointed Royal stag as their crest, which has become the iconic emblem of The Dalmore. Their motto is 'fortune favours the brave'.

Defining Distinctiveness

Each story defines its distinctiveness by finding a way to connect to the explorer. The key narrative themes appear to be identity, affinity or profiling the consumer.

Identity denotes how the consumer sees him or herself through self-expression. Some connect to heritage, whether it's their own or someone else's. To images of strength and tradition, like the Viking stock of the Orkney or favouring the brave of Dalmore. Some relate to the identity of the 'outlier', as in the case of Bruichladdich, or to mood, romantic notion or landscape, such as the hills and glens of the Highlands or the peat-laden bogs and salty air of the Hebrides.

Affinity is about associating the consumer to a 'community' of others who share a similar interest, whether a group, location or product. Ardbeg's outposts and embassy groups are examples, as well as Laphroaig's circle of friends with their honorary lifetime lease to a square foot of land.

On an informal level, affinity is about joining local tasting clubs or aligning to organizations like The Scotch Malt Whisky Society.

Profiling is when others attempt to place consumers in categories. Targeting millennials' or hipsters as peaty smoky types is one example, rather than profiling them as lighter and citrusier types. Another is suggesting that women express their individuality by drinking their single malt neat, rather than with cubes or soda.

Regardless of categories, a good narrative is emotive, memorable and willingly shared through social media and other forms of cultural dissemination. For the 'discriminating' whisky explorer, the narrative should cut through the market hysteria of consumerism and other cultural distractions and enable one to trust what they hear (or read) as true. Here, the story must demonstrate relevance by connecting to identity or affinity for the consumer/explorer to take notice.

The challenge in a geo-expanding market is redefining the 'consumer', especially one that no longer fits the monolithic Western European profile. The 'postmodern' consumer is more likely polylithic and drawn to simulacra, through visual interpretation, emphasizing cultural value rather than story. In this context, whisky is a commodity, a must-have, a signifier of prestige. But with prestige, there are those who find ways to replicate and black-market the product to offset costs and demand.

The expectation is that there will be more replication, not less, and this will lead to market 'blindness' and potential health-related issues for those who indulge. Market blindness is also a huge concern for collectors who will no longer trust the high-end whiskies they are buying.

Notwithstanding the industry challenges, we expect that there is enough market oomph to maintain current market expansion. However, the question is when will market expansion cease to continue?

We know that in the late 1800s, the 'Pattison Crash' was precipitated by greed; the 1930s and 40s by war and religious intolerance; and the 1970s and 80's by changing demographics of a baby boomer generation that was now old enough to drink but no longer interested in being the image of their parents. This time, will it be due to cultural contraction, another economic recession or some unbeknownst market disruption? And, how will it be mitigated or possibly avoided?

The current industry focus has been on branding, innovation and experimentation. But if innovation or experimentation is what we can expect, where does tradition and integrity fit?

For those we talked to, we learned that for some they liked that single malt whisky was trendy and fit with their lifestyle choices. They saw themselves continuing with their whisky choices until something changes. But for others it wasn't about trends or enticing narratives, as their interest in whisky came to them through self-discovery - some with friends and others alone. Intrigued and curious, to the extent that they were able to find a deeper sense of what a dram offers. They knew that beyond the myths and lore, a good single malt Scotch was something special to pair with their moods, share with friends or with activities that made pairing enjoyable.

We also learned that one cannot rely on old ways of doing things or stick with old images of who we think we are or would like to be. Similarly, the whisky industry cannot be stuck in its own drive for profitability and economic gain or worry about whether they will continue to be the whisky of choice with the emergence of new whisky entrepreneurs.

We all must be willing to go back to that place of being curious that allows for new core experiences and new ways of doing things, while maintaining the richness and quality of the dram. This is when we rediscover our sense of authenticness.

So, does one's notion of authenticness fit with the stories the distilleries tell? Possibly. Perhaps, it is more than simply aligning to the distillery narratives. A true pairing with the consumer/explorer is when the distiller is also valuing authenticness, by demonstrating less concern about cosmetics (such as chill filtration or adding E150a to colour their whisky) and more concerned about maintaining the artistic expression that emboldens their spirit.

Figure 24 Edinburgh

One could surmise that single malt Scotch is bigger than Scotland. In most cases, the new make spirit has been paired with Sherry butts from Spain, Bourbon barrels from the United States, Port casks from Portugal, numerous wine casks from France and Italy, Caribbean rum from Cuba, and ice wine casks from Canada. And, the list of unique cask pairings keeps growing. This makes Scotch universal. What keeps the single malt Scotch a step beyond other whiskies is the structure and standards maintained by industry regulations, matched by high consumer expectations for single malt Scotch over other whiskies or blends.

The true essence of the single malt Scotch is in the expression of what is offered and the tradition in which it is produced. Underlying the essence is and should continue to be a willingness on the part of the industry to listen to the consumer/explorer to maintain their trust and loyalty. Authenticness is about defining who we are, not being defined by others. For those who have discovered this – we raise a dram.

Baying at the Moon

> *A group of guys from Lund, a small community on northern Sunshine Coast of British Columbia, would get together at each full moon to play crokinole, drink Scotch and bay at the moon. This went on for years. Now that many of the original group have passed on, their sons are taking up the tradition. Some may think this is good and others may question why. Our sense of who we are and where we are heading lies in knowing where we have been. Whether we choose to bay at the moon or not, the importance is embracing the spirit within.*

Figure 25 Baying at the moon

Medicinal Proof?

In September 2016, Grace Jones, who had turned 110 years of age, declared: "Whisky is very good for you. I started having a nightly tot of it when I turned 50, so I've been having it every night for the last 60 years and I certainly have no intention of stopping now". "My doctor said: 'keep up with the whisky Grace, it's good for your heart'." Her whisky of choice is Famous Grouse. In September 2018, she turned 112 years of age and is still tipping back her nightly tot.

Post Scriptum

Figure 26 Sir Walter Scott

> *The Monument is in honour of Sir Walter Scott, a poet and historical novelist, who helped heal the fissure that destabilized Scottish society following the Battle of Culloden and laid the groundwork for legalized distilling of Highland malt. In 1822, at a gala honoring King George IV, the first British monarch to visit Scotland in 170 years, he re-introduced Highland tartan pageantry to Scottish society and served illicit Highland whisky (Glenlivet) in toasting the King. The Monument was designed by George Meikle Kemp (1795 - 1844), who was* not *an architect, but a carpenter - a true blue collar and scholar.*

APPENDIX

New Distilleries in Scotland

Due to market demand, new distilleries are opening in Scotland at an unprecedented rate. Numerous distilleries are in production with new malts and, in some cases, other distilled products, such as gin, rye, rum and vodka. They too will need to find their market niche. Is there still room in the current set of narratives for more outliers, traditionalists, heritage types and other identity seekers? Something to look forward to.

The Lowlands

Kingsbarns is a rebuilt dilapidated farm house near St. Andrews in Fife.

Annandale in Dumfries and Galloway at one time was owned by Johnny Walker back in the late 1800s.

Inchdairnie west of Glenrothes in Fife.

Daftmill a farmhouse distillery in Fife.

Ailsa Bay in Girvan, Ayrshire.

Glasgow Distillery located in the Hillington Business Park in Glasgow;

Lindores Abbey in Fife, which was the location of Friar John Cor's written record back in 1494 where records indicated that he was instructed by King James IV to make "aqua vitae, VIII bolls of malt".

The Clydeside Distillery is another new distillery in Glasgow.

The Borders Distillery, situated in Hawick, will be the first legal distillery in the Borders in over 180 years.

Speyside

Ballindallach in Banffshire.

Dalmunach is built on the site of the former Imperial Distillery in Banffshire.

Eastern Highlands

Roseisle in Morayshire.

Lone Wolf, outside of Aberdeen will offer, besides malt, a range of grain, rye and Bourbon, as well as vodka, gin and rum.

Isle of Raasay east of the Isle of Skye in Raasay.

Western_Highlands

Ardnamurchan in Glenbeg, Argyll, just north of the Isle of Mull, makes it the most western distillery on the mainland.

Ncn'ean located on the Drimnin Estate overlooking the Isle of Mull.

Arbikie in Arbroath, Angus.

Central_Highlands

Brora across the road from Clynelish will re-open in 2020.

Southern_Highlands

Strathearn is viewed as Scotland's first micro-distillery and is in Methven.

Northern_Highlands

Dornoch, a converted 135-year-old fire station, Dornoch, Sutherland.

Islands

Harris located in Tarbert on the Isle of Harris.

Torabhaig is the second distillery located on the Isle of Skye.

Islay

Ardnahoe, located between Caol Ila and Bunnahabhain on the north-east coast, will be offering casks in addition to bottled products.

Port Ellen – expected to be re-opened and in full production by 2020

With more to come!

WHISKY ALPHABET

Alc/vol or ABV – Alcohol by volume. A standard measure to determine how much alcohol (ethanol) is contained within a given volume of whisky (40% - 68%). Typically, whisky is between 40% – 46% abv, with 40% abv equal to 40% alcohol and 60% water.

Ageing – The maturation of whisky in an oak barrel or cask. Whisky must be aged a minimum of 3 years, but typically aged 10 years or more. The ageing process is presumed to stop when the whisky is bottled.

Alligator Char – Refers to the cracked shiny texture on the inside of the barrel that is left by the charring process. There are four levels of charring with the 4th level – known as the alligator char producing the most pronounced alligator effect.

American Oak – Also known as Quercus Alba. A type of American hardwood used for casks. The staves are usually thicker than those used for casks made from European Oak.

Angel's Share – During cask maturation, approximately 1.5-2% of the whisky is lost each year due to evaporation.

Barley – The cereal grain used as the key ingredient in the production of malt whisky.

Blended Whisky – A mixture of malt whisky and grain whisky.

Blended Malt - A blend of different single malts from more than one distillery.

Bonded – By law, whisky must be stored for 3 years under the control of Customs and Excise, before it can legally be called whisky. In practice, whisky is usually stored on average about 10 years or more.

Bothie - A small single room building or hidden underground structure in the Scottish Highlands where illicit distilling was practiced.

Bourbon – An American whiskey, distilled from a mash having at least 51 percent corn, in addition to malt and rye, and aged in American oak barrels.

Brewing – Process by which wort is fermented with yeast in a washback to produce a Wash that is roughly 8% abv, which is then distilled to make whisky.

Butt - Is a large cask for maturing alcoholic beverages, made from oak, with capacity for 500 litres – roughly twice that of a hogshead. Butts are often used for Sherry maturation.

Céad míle fáilte! (Kay-od mee-leh foyl-cha) – Hundred thousand welcomes!

Caramel Colouring - Spirit Caramel, often referred to as E150a, is a tasteless liquid used to ensure that whisky has a consistent colour when it is bottled.

Cask - A wooden vessel usually made of oak, where whisky is stored in order to mature. Common practice is to age whisky in casks originally used for Bourbon (American Oak) or Sherry (European Oak) to impart character to the spirit.

Cask Strength - Whisky taken straight from the cask, often greater than 60% and bottled at the same strength without being diluted with water.

Charring – Charring the inside of the barrel darkens the wood and caramelizes some of the sugars in the Oak, which affects both the colour and flavour of the whisky. Charring is done to change the nature of the oak itself, to yield the best possible reaction between wood and whisky.

Chill filtered – Whisky that is cooled (0 degree Celsius for single malt) and filtered to remove fatty acids, esters and other volatile compounds that creates a cloudiness in the whisky when cooled.

Coffey Still – Also known as a patent or continuous still consists of two columns and acts like a series of pot stills, producing vapour with an alcohol content of about 96% abv. It is used for producing grain whisky used in blends.

Condenser - A copper tube from the lyne arm of the still, surrounded by many small copper pipes which are fed with cool water for cooling spirit vapours. The spirit vapours condense quickly with maximum copper contact.

Congener – Chemical compounds (impurities) produced during fermentation that gives whisky its flavour and aroma. Congeners include esters, acids, aldehydes, methanol and other alcohols.

Cooper - A highly-skilled crafts-person who makes and repairs the casks for whisky maturation.

Cooperage – Where barrels or casks are made.

Cut – When a young whisky has been distilled in the spirit still, the distiller looks for the foreshots, the cut is the middle part which is collected and filled into casks for maturation, and the feints which are collected at the end of the distillation process. Foreshots and feints are re-distilled while the middle is transferred to the casks for maturing.

Deoch en' Doris (gee-ock en doris) – one for the door before leaving.

Distillation – Is the process by which whisky is produced by separating the components or substances from a liquid mixture by selective boiling and condensation. Single malt whisky is distilled twice with the first distillation in the Wash Still producing the low wines and the second distillation taking place in the Spirit Still.

Draff - The spent grain left in the mash-tun after the wort has been siphoned off.

Dram - A term commonly used to describe a small drink of whisky. In England it is 25 ml pour and 35 ml in Scotland. In North America the standard whisky pour is 30 ml.

Dunnage - A traditional type of warehouse made of stone or brick where casks are stacked on top of each other - no more than three high in a warehouse. A dunnage warehouse is usually earth floored with good air circulation and higher humidity levels.

Ester – A sweet-smelling congener in whisky. Esters can be vanilla, pineapple and buttery notes found in the whisky.

European Oak – Also referred to as Quercus Robur. A type of hardwood used for casks that contributes rich, red berry, spicy, tannin, flavours to the whisky. The staves are usually thicker than those used for casks made from American Oak.

Feints – Also known as tails, or after-shots. The weak and final portion of the spirit collected after the second distillation process. The Feints are added to the next batch of low wines and re-distilled.

Fermentation - The process by which yeast is added to the barley extract. The process takes place in a wash back and results in a type of "beer".

Fáilte (foyl-chuh) - Welcome

Finish - A term used to describe the longevity of flavours lingering in the mouth after tasting a whisky.

Foreshots - Are the first part of the distillation process in the spirit still. The foreshots (or heads) are very high in alcohol with about 80% abv that contain many volatile compounds. Foreshots are collected together with the feints to be returned to the spirit still to be redistilled.

Glencairn glass - A tulip-shaped glass used to sniff and taste whisky. It has a narrow opening to enable the fragrance to be concentrated in the nostrils.

Grain Whisky – Made from any grain and usually distilled in a continuous or Coffey still.

Milling – A grinding process where malted barley is ground to make grist (70%), husks 20%, and flour (10%).

Grist – Is produced from the grinding of malted barley during the milling process used for making whisky.

Heads – Also known as fore shots which is the spirit collected after the second distilling.

Heart of the Run - It is the second part of the distilled alcohol from the spirit sill - between the Foreshot and the Feints - which is collected, ready to be matured into whisky.

Highlands - Is the biggest region and therefore embraces a wide variety of malts that are considered warm and rounded with spicy notes. Defining where to draw the line between the Highlands and Lowlands has shifted over the years. The Wash

Act of 1784 drew a line across Scotland between Dunoon in the west to Dundee in the east. Then, in 1797, an intermediate area was defined which shifted the Highland line so that it ran from Lochgilphead to Findhorn.

Hogshead - A 250 litre barrel used to store whisky

Independent Bottling - An independent bottling is a whisky that has been bottled by someone other than the distillery that produced it.

Irish Whiskey – A malt whiskey produced from barley in the same way as Scotch, except it is generally triple distilled.

Kiln - Both the oven and the buildings which house the oven are called the kiln. The process in the kiln is called kilning and the purpose of kilning is to arrest malt growth by drying the malt down to approx. 4.5% moisture.

Kilning – A heat process by which the malted barley is dried to stop the germination process. Kilns can be fired using a variety of heat sources. Traditionally, peat was used which imparted a smoky flavour into the whisky.

Lignin – Complex molecule found in oak. Lignin in the wood helps add vanillin to the spirit (offering vanilla and marzipan-like flavours).

Low wines - The weak spirits resulting from the first run of the still from the fermented mash. The name low comes from the low strength of about 22- 24% abv.

Lyne Arm (or Lye Pipe) - This is the pipe that extends from the neck of the still and where the spirit vapours are transported to be condensed back into liquid. The angle of the pipe influences the character of the whisky as it can promote or diminish the amount of contact between vapour and copper, which results in a light or heavy body. Stills with a lye pipe that angles upwards allow greater reflux, where conveners flow back into the still giving a lighter spirit. Stills with a downward sloping arm or pipe tend to produce a heavier spirit as there is less reflux involved.

Marriage – A vatting or blending of two or more casks from the same distillery.

Malting – The process by which barley is first wet and then spread on the floor of the malting house. The barley germinates, allowing a chemical change to take place where the starch in the grain turns to sugar, which later produces alcohol. At the end of the process, the barley is dried in a heated kiln to stop the germination process.

Malting Floor – Floor of the malting house where raw barley is soaked in water and spread to germinate.

Mashing – Process by which the milled malted Barley is mixed with hot water and progressively heated to obtain a sugary liquid called 'wort'.

Mash Tun - A large circular vat used in the mashing process to convert the starches in crushed grains into sugars for fermentation. Most mash tuns are insulated to maintain a constant temperature and most have a false bottom and spigot so that the sparging process can be done in the same vessel.

Maturation – The ageing of whisky in an oak barrel or cask. Whisky is aged a minimum of 3 or more years. The ageing process stops when the whisky is bottled, unlike wine which continues to mature in the bottle.

Middle cut – The ideal portion of spirit collected as a result of the distillation process.

Milling - At the mill, malted barley is loaded into the mill hopper and goes through the mill where sets of rollers crack the husks and grind the malt. It should produce 10% flour, 20% husk and 70% grit. These proportions are checked very thoroughly because if too fine, the mash tun will not drain quickly enough. If too coarse, the liquor will drain too fast and maximum extraction will not occur.

Monkey Shoulder – A medical condition resulting from turning barley by hand on a malting floor. The condition causes one arm to hang lower than the other. 'Monkey Shoulder' is also the name of a blended malt whisky that consists of a mix of three Speyside single malts.

Mouthfeel – The texture of the whisky in the mouth. The texture can be soft and velvety to creamy and oily to waxy or prickly

New Make - Spirit freshly distilled and of high strength with around 70% abv. New make spirit is ready to be filled into casks. Most distilleries dilute the spirit to 63.5% abv before it is filled into casks to mature. New make becomes whisky after maturing in the cask for a minimum of 3 years.

New Oak – refers to a virgin barrel. Bourbon is always stored in new oak.

Nosing - The process used to identify different aromas by smelling the whisky.

Palate – Flavour and feel of whisky in the mouth.

Patent Still – Another word for Coffey or Continuous Still as noted above.

Peated whisky – whisky which has been made using barley dried in a peat fired kiln. It typically has a smoky flavour.

Phenols or PPM - The abbreviation for Parts per Million – the scientific measurement for showing the amount of phenols present in the malt used to make whisky. Phenols are located in the malt from the burning of peat. The phenolic content of the malt does not necessarily correlate with the phenolic content of the final matured whisky.

Pot Still – A type of copper distillation vessel, resembling a large kettle, commonly used for the distillation of whisky. Pot-bellied in shape, with a long swan like neck, heat is applied directly to the pot. The alcoholic vapour rises up, through the neck and into the condenser.

Proof - A standardised measurement to determine the alcoholic strength. Originally, a small amount of gunpowder was used to determine if the mixture was of high or low proof. If the powder did not ignite, the mixture had too much water and the proof was considered low. Spirit that is 100 degrees proof equals to 57.1% alcohol so 70% proof equal to 40% alcohol according to the British definition.

Rack House – A structure where whisky casks are stored on their sides and stacked several stories high during the aging process.

Reflux - When pot stills are used for distillation, the process of vapour condensing within the still and then re-boiling is called "reflux". The amount of reflux is influenced by the shape of the still and by the direction of the lyne arm (lye pipe). When the lyne arm angles upwards, more reflux is created. Therefore, a still with an upward sloping lyne arm will have the most reflux resulting in increased copper contact, giving the lightest spirit, whereas a downwards sloping lyne arm creates a heavier spirit.

Rye - A type of whisky, made mostly in North America.

Single cask – used to describe whisky where the entire contents of the bottle have come from a single cask.

Single Malt – A bottling of whisky that comes from one distillery and is not diluted with grain whisky.

Slàinte Mhath - (slahnje va), with a response of "Slàinte Mhòr" (slahnje vor) - means "Good Health ... Great Health," almost exclusively used when drinking whisky.

Spirit Safe – Usually glass-walled and brass bound that is found in all distilleries with several glass vessels that act as receptacles for the distillate. The spirit safe links the stills to the holding tanks. Traditionally, it is padlocked and under the control of Customs and Excise to prevent anyone siphoning off the new make spirit to avoid paying duty on it. It has instruments, such as a thermometer and hydrometer, for the distiller to analyse and manage the spirit coming out of the spirit stills.

Spirit Still - A pot still where low wines, the foreshots and feints from the previous distillation, are mixed and heated to produce the spirit which is later filled into oak casks to mature. The spirit still is used for the second, occasionally third, distillation in the process. The spirit still is usually, with a few exceptions, smaller than the wash still.

Tails – Also known as feints, or after-shots. The weak and final portion of the spirit collected after the second distillation process. The Feints are added to the next batch of low wines and re-distilled.

Tannin – An astringent chemical found in oak that adds astringency or "dryness" when tasting whisky. During the maturation process, tannins help remove unpleasant sulphury notes.

Toasting - A similar process to charring of casks but less aggressive due to the more porous nature of European oak.

Triple distilled – Auchentoshan Distillery in Scotland and most distilleries in Ireland choose to distill their whisky three times to achieve a higher, cleaner spirit.

Unpeated malt - Malted barley that has been dried in a kiln without peat, thus with very little or no phenolic content.

Uisge Beatha – (oosh-ga-beh-ha), The Scots Gaelic term for Aqua Vitae, also known as "Water of Life". The word "whisky" derives from "uisge" which over time was abbreviated to whisky.

Vanillin – Organic compound found in oak that provides vanilla-like flavour to the whisky.

Valinch - A large pipette used to sample spirit from a cask.

Vatted Malt/Vatting – A blended malt that uses only single malt whiskies

Washback – A large vessel, often made of Oregon pine or stainless steel, used for fermenting the wort and the yeast into Wash.

Wash – A fermented wort or type of crude beer produced during the fermentation process, which is the distilled to make whisky.

Wash Still - The first pot still used in distillation where the Wash from the Washback is distilled.

Wood Finish – Whisky is sometimes matured in a second cask to finish it with additional flavour. Common finishes are Sherry, Madeira and Burgundy.

Worm Tub – A coiled copper tube (worm) submerged within a large tub used to condense the gaseous alcohol vapours coming off the still. They're usually seen in large wooden or cast-iron vats at Glenkinchie, Dalwhinnie and Talisker. The worms are used to slowly condense spirit vapours with minimum copper contact producing a rich spirit character.

Wort – A sugary liquid produced from the Mash Tun during the mashing process containing high amounts of soluble sugars from the grist dissolved in hot water. The liquid drawn from the Mash Tun will later be fermented with the addition of yeast.

Yeast - Yeast is used in the fermentation process to feed on the sugar and produces carbon dioxide and ethyl alcohol.

PRONUNCIATION GUIDE OF SCOTTISH DISTILLERIES

Aberfeldy [ah-bur-fell-dee]

Aberlour [ah-bur-lower]

Allt-a-Bhainne [alt-a-vain]

Ardbeg [ard-beg]

Ardmore [ard-moor]

Arran [ar-ran]

Auchetoshan [ock-en-tosh-en]

Auchroisk [ar-thrusk]

Aultmore [ault-moor]

Balblair [bal-blair]

Balmenach [bal-may-nack]

Balvenie [bal-ven-ee]

Ben Nevis [ben-nev-iss]

Benriach [ben-ree-ack]

Benrinnes [ben-rin-ess]

Benromach [ben-ro-mack]

Bladnoch [blad-nock]

Blair Athol [blair-ath-ull]

Bowmore [bow-moor]

Braeval [bre-vaal]

Bruichladdich [brook-lad-dee]

Bunnahabhain [buh-nah-hav-enn]

Caol Ila [cull-eel-a]

Cardhu [car-doo]

Clynelish [cline-leash]

Cragganmore [crag-an-moor]

Craigellachie [craig-ell-ack-ee]

Dailuaine [dall-yoo-an]

Dalmore [dal-moor]

Dalwhinnie [dal-whin-nay]

Deanston [deen-stun]

Dufftown [duff-town]

Edradour [ed-ra-dow-er]

Fettercairn [fett-er-cairn]

Glenallachie [glen-alla-key]

Glenburgie [glen-bur-gee]

Glencadam [glen-ka-dam]

Glendronach [glen-dro-nack]

Glendullan [glen-dull-an]

Glen Elgin [glen-el-gin]

Glenfarclas [glen-fark-lass]

Glenfiddich [glen-fidd-ick]

Glen Garioch [glen-gee-ree]

Glenglassaugh [glen-glass-ock]

Glengoyne [glen-goyn]

Glen Grant [glen-grant]

Glen Gyle [glen-gyle]

Glen Keith [glen-keeth]

Glenkinchie [glen-kin-chee]

Glenlivet [glen-liv-it]

Glenlossie [glen-loss-ay]

Glenmorangie [glen-mor-run-jee]

Glen Moray [glen-mur-ree]

Glen Ord [glen-ord]

Glenrothes [glen-roth-iss]

Glen Scotia [glen-sko-sha]

Glen Spey [glen-spay]

Glentauchers [glen-tock-ers]

Glenturret [glen-turr-et]

Highland Park [highland-park]

Inchgower [inch-gow-er]

Jura [joo-rah]

Kilchoman [kil-ho-man]

Kininvie [kin-in-vee]

Knockando [nock-an-doo]

Knockdhu [nock-doo]

Lagavulin [lah-gah-voo-lin]

Laphroaig [lah-froyg]

Linkwood [link-wood]

Loch Lomond [lock-low-mund]

Longmorn [long-morn]

Macallan [mack-al-un]

Macduff [mack-duff]

Mannochmore [man-ock-moor]

Miltonduff [Mill-ton-duff]

Mortlach [mort-lack]

Oban [oh-bun]

Pulteney [poolt-knee]

Royal Brackla [royal brack-la]

Royal Lochnagar [royal-lock-nah-gar]

Scapa [ska-pa]

Speyburn [spey-burn]

Speyside [spey-side]

Springbank [spring-bank]

Strathisla [strath-eye-la]

Strathmill [strath-mill]

Talisker [tal-iss-ker]

Tamdhu [tam-doo]

Tamnavulin [tam-na-voo-li]

Teaninich [tee-ni-nick]

Tobermory [tow-bur-mo-ray]

Tomatin [to-mat-in]

Tomintoul [tom-in-towel]

Tormore [tor-more]

Tullibardine [tully-bar-din]

ABOUT THE AUTHORS

Adam Drummond – is a certified automotive service technician who has been fixing cars for a living for the past 13 years. Although new car technology is now computer driven, highly intricate and complex, he claims it is still very much a blue collar job.

Figure 27 Blue Collar

When he is not working, he is a Scottish Highland Games Heavy Events athlete (yes, he tosses cabers and stones), coach and trainer. Working 10 hours a day, raising two daughters with his beautiful wife, lifting weights and training for competitions keeps him rather busy.

Gregory Cran – is a university principal and former Dean and Associate Professor. He has a PhD in Public Administration with a focus on ethno-political conflict. He worked as a consultant for the World Bank Institute and United Nations Development Programme and has taught and lectured internationally as well.

Figure 28 Scholar

His book publishing includes *Negotiating Buck Naked: Doukhobors, Public Policy and Conflict Resolution* (2006) UBC Press.

He and Wendy have travelled to Scotland numerous times, visiting subterranean relatives, learning about their enjoined past and experiencing the essence of what Scotland has to offer.

RE-SOURCES

Banks, Iain (2004). Raw Spirit: In Search of the Perfect Dram. Arrow Books, UK.

Barnard, Alfred (1887). The Whisky Distilleries of the United Kingdom, London: Harper. (Reprinted by Lochar Publishing & Mainstream Publishing of Edinburgh in 1987).

Brander, Michael (1974). A Guide to Scotch Whisky. Johnston & Bacon.

Broom, Dave (2000). Handbook of Whisky. London: Hamlyn.

De Kergommeaux, Davin (2017). Canadian Whisky: The New Portable Expert 2nd Edition. Penguin Random House.

Devine, T M (1994). Clanship to Crofters' War: The Social Transformation of the Scottish Highlands. Manchester University Press.

Devine, T.M. (2006). The Scottish Nation: 1700-2007. Penguin Books.

Duthie, G.G., Pedersen, M.W., Gardner, P.T., Morrice, P.C., Jenkinson, A McE., McPhail, D.B. & Steele, G.M. (1998). The effect of whisky and wine consumption on total phenol content and antioxidant capacity of plasma from healthy volunteers. European Journal of Clinical Nutrition 52, 733-736.

Fry, Michael (2005). Wild Scots: Four Hundred Years of Highland History. John Murray Publisher.

Hollinshed, Raphael (1577). Chronicles of England, Scotland and Ireland.

Jackson, Michael (1991). The World Guide to Whisky. Dorling Kindersley, London.

Jackson, Michael (1989). Michael Jackson's Malt Whisky Companion. Dorling Kindersley, London.

Jackson, Michael (1989). Michael Jackson's Complete Guide to Single Malt Scotch. Dorling Kindersley, London.

Jackson, Michael (2010). Michael Jackson's Complete Guide to Single Malt Scotch (6th ed.) DK Publishing

Marshall, Robb. J. (1950). Scotch Whisky: An Illustrated Guide. W. & R. Chambers, London and Edinburgh.

Murray, Jim (1997). The Complete Guide to Whiskey: Selecting, Comparing, and Drinking the World's Great Whiskeys. Triumph Books.

Murray, Jim (2018). Whisky Bible 2019: The World's Leading Whisky Guide. Dram Good Books Ltd.

MacLean, Charles (2010). Whiskypedia: A Compendium of Scottish Whisky. Skyhorse Publishing.

MacLean, Charles (2015). Spirit of Place: Scotland's Great Whisky Distilleries. Chicago Review Press.

"The Scotch Whisky Regulations 2009". UK Parliament. 2009. Retrieved 30 April 2018.

Malt Whisky Yearbook 2018: the facts, the people, the news, the stories. MagDig Media Ltd. England.

Photo Credits

Figures 1, 3, 5, 6, 7, 8, 13, 15, 18, 19, 24, 26 photos by Gregory Cran

Figures 10, 16, 21, 22, 23, 25 photos by Wendy Drummond

Figure 14 by permission of Charles MacLean

Figure 17 photo by Steven Grover

Figure 20 photo by Dan Baxter

Figure 27 photo by Brandy Drummond

Figure 28 photo by Jennifer Dodd

ACKNOWLEDGEMENTS

First and foremost, we wish to acknowledge Wendy Drummond (mother and wife of Blue Collar and Scholar) for both her brilliance and diligence in keeping us in line, managing the website and its analytics, preparing budgets and posters and a myriad of other tasks, including researching and editing, and all things related to this project. We simply could not have done it without her help.

We would like to thank Brandy (Adam's wife) and Kaelyn and Kenzie (daughters/granddaughters) for all their love and support throughout.

We would also like to thank Chris Drummond for his stories, such as soaking his harmonica in a glass of whisky and his yellow tux that made us laugh. We would also like to thank him for his edits as well.

A huge thank you to Dan and Ellen Baxter for boldly venturing into the world of whisky to acquire a repertoire of whiskies that the ardent collector would envy. Dan allowed us to open our world to unique whisky tastings that have been mind blowing at best.

A special mention to Chef John D. Walls from Culinary Magic and his Modern Peasant Restaurant in Powell River, British Columbia for his amazing culinary pairings and for the inspiration and creativity he imbues with each dish.

And, a special thank you to Leon Webb, Master Distiller at Shelter Point Distillery on northern Vancouver Island, and his wife Lydia Fisher for helping us with the edits and for enhancing our understanding and appreciation of the distillation process. Shelter Point has produced a new range of award-winning Canadian whiskies. (Jim Murray described their Artisanal Cask Strength whisky as "brilliant" giving it a rating score of 91.)

We would also like to thank Nicole Narbonne for her help with the cover design and to the amazing Charles MacLean for his comments and suggestions and for sharing his own insights and thoughts on the alchemy of tasting. Truly appreciated!

TASTING NOTES

Single Malt Whisky:

Nose:

Taste:

Finish:

Single Malt Whisky:

Nose:

Taste:

Finish:

Single Malt Whisky:

Nose:

Taste:

Finish:

Single Malt Whisky:

Nose:

Taste:

Finish:

Single Malt Whisky:

Nose:

Taste:

Finish:

Single Malt Whisky:

Nose:

Taste:

Finish:

Single Malt Whisky:

Nose:

Taste:

Finish:

Single Malt Whisky:

Nose:

Taste:

Finish:

www.ingramcontent.com/pod-product-compliance
Ingram Content Group UK Ltd.
Pitfield, Milton Keynes, MK11 3LW, UK
UKHW021830270726
14058UKWH00001B/63